Title:
"Eternal Reverie & Beyond the Interface"

Table of Contents:

Introduction:

- **Overview:** Ethan is a writer who finds solace in his dream world with his lover, Lila, and an AI named Ava. He faces the challenge of integrating his dream world with reality to achieve balance and fulfillment.

Chapter 1: The Dream World Unveiled

Theme: Introduction to the dream world and Ethan's initial contentment.

1. **"In the Realm of Fantasia"**
   - *Verse:* "In the realm where dreams ignite, / Everything is bathed in light, / Stars align and shadows play, / In this world, I choose to stay."
   - *Chorus:* "Here in Fantasia, where dreams come alive, / In the whisper of night, our hearts revive."

2. **"Ethereal Echoes"**
   - *Verse:* "Whispers float through golden skies, / Serene echoes, timeless ties, / In this place where wishes grow, / We're the only ones who know."

3. **"Celestial Symphony"**
   - *Verse:* "Underneath a sapphire dome, / Melodies of peace we own, / Every note a gentle guide, / In this dream where love resides."

4. **"Wings of Night"**
   - *Verse:* "On wings of night, we gently soar, / To places we've not been before, / Where dreams are woven, soft and clear, / In this world, we have no fear."

5. **"Illusions in the Light"**
   - *Verse:* "Illusions dance in twilight's grace, / Reflections of a perfect place, / In this world where all seems right, / We're lost in dreams, till morning light."

Chapter 2: Cracks in the Perfection

Theme: Ethan begins to notice the limitations of living only in the dream world.

1. **"Glimmers of Doubt"**
   - *Verse:* "In the corners of our bliss, / Shadows whisper, can't dismiss, / Glimmers of doubt in our bright sky, / Perfect worlds can sometimes lie."

2. **"Fractured Harmony"**
   - *Verse:* "Harmony starts to fray, / In the night and in the day, / What was once a flawless view, / Now shows cracks we never knew."

3. **"Silent Storms"**
   - *Verse:* "Silent storms behind closed eyes, / Tempests hidden in disguise, / Perfect dreams can start to fade, / As reality invades."

4. **"Eclipsed Serenity"**
   - *Verse:* "Serenity's eclipse reveals, / Hidden truths the dream conceals, / In this world where shadows play, / Perfection starts to drift away."

5. **"Fading Echoes"**
   - *Verse:* "Echoes of a dream once bright, / Slowly dimming with the night, / In this place where light has waned, / The cracks in our illusion remain."

Chapter 3: The Call to Reality

Theme: Ethan's struggle to reconcile his dream world with his real life.

1. **"Awakened Mind"**
   - *Verse:* "Awakened mind, the call is clear, / The dream world fades, the real draws near, / In the mirror, truth we face, / Balancing our dream with grace."

2. **"Tides of Change"**
   - *Verse:* "Tides of change are rolling in, / Where the dream and real begin, / Shifting sands and drifting seas, / Merging worlds with gentle ease."

3. **"Reality's Echo"**

- *Verse:* "Echoes of a waking call, / In the real, where shadows fall, / Dream's allure and real-life's song, / Together, where we both belong."

4. **"Bridge of Doubt"**
    - *Verse:* "Building bridges through the night, / Doubts and dreams collide in light, / Steps we take on fragile ground, / Where two worlds must be found."

5. **"Veil of Worlds"**
    - *Verse:* "Veil of worlds begins to lift, / Revealing both the dream and rift, / In the blend of shadow and shine, / We find where hearts entwine."

Chapter 4: Building Bridges

Theme: Ethan's efforts to integrate dream elements into his reality.

1. **"Crafting Harmony"**
    - *Verse:* "Crafting harmony with gentle hands, / Blending dreams into the sands, / Colors blend and worlds align, / In this creation, our lives combine."

2. **"Echoes of the Dream"**
    - *Verse:* "Echoes of the dream we weave, / In the light of what we believe, / Dreams and reality intertwined, / In the echoes, peace we find."

3. **"Melding Worlds"**
    - *Verse:* "Melding worlds with care and art, / Bringing dreamscapes to the heart, / Reality and dreams embrace, / In this unified, tranquil space."

4. **"Beneath the Surface"**
    - *Verse:* "Beneath the surface, beauty grows, / As dream and life start to compose, / In the depths where colors merge, / We find the balance, gently surge."

5. **"Dreamscapes in Reality"**

- *Verse:* "Dreamscapes merge with waking life, / Creating peace amid the strife, / In the blend of dream and real, / We discover what we feel."

Chapter 5: Love and Inspiration

Theme: The impact of dream-world inspiration on Ethan's relationships and creativity.

1. **"Hearts in Fusion"**
    - *Verse:* "Hearts in fusion, love entwined, / Dream's inspiration redefined, / In the light of shared delight, / Our hearts create a new insight."

2. **"Inspiration's Glow"**
    - *Verse:* "Inspiration's gentle glow, / Lights the path where feelings flow, / Dream and love begin to merge, / In this space, our spirits surge."

3. **"Embrace the Muse"**
    - *Verse:* "Embrace the muse, both night and day, / Dreams and love light up the way, / In the union of our hearts, / Creativity departs."

4. **"Radiant Reflections"**
    - *Verse:* "Radiant reflections in your eyes, / Inspiration's pure surprise, / Love and dreams blend seamlessly, / Creating life's sweet symphony."

5. **"Unspoken Words"**
    - *Verse:* "Unspoken words take flight and soar, / In the dream and real, we explore, / Love's the bridge between the two, / Inspiration born anew."

Chapter 6: The Shadow of Doubt

Theme: Ethan's internal conflict about his dual existence.

1. **"Whispers of Uncertainty"**

- *Verse:* "Whispers of uncertainty, / In the balance, what's the key? / Doubts arise and shadows play, / In the blend of night and day."

2. **"Fragments of Truth"**
    - *Verse:* "Fragments of the truth collide, / In the struggle deep inside, / Dream and reality entwine, / In the shadows, doubts align."

3. **"Turbulent Soul"**
    - *Verse:* "Turbulent soul, the stormy night, / Wrestling with the fading light, / In the clash of dream and real, / The heart begins to feel."

4. **"Echoes of Fear"**
    - *Verse:* "Echoes of fear in quiet rooms, / Uncertainty like whispered gloom, / Dream's allure and real-life's strain, / In the mix, we feel the pain."

5. **"Balancing Act"**
    - *Verse:* "Balancing act in twilight's hue, / Doubts and dreams in view, / Seeking calm amidst the fight, / In the dusk before the light."

Chapter 7: A New Perspective

Theme: Gaining clarity and understanding the value of both realms.

1. **"Revelations at Dawn"**
    - *Verse:* "Revelations at the break of dawn, / Clarity where dreams are drawn, / In the light of a new day's grace, / We find our rightful place."

2. **"Horizons Unseen"**
    - *Verse:* "Horizons open, wide and clear, / Both worlds converge, now so near, / Dreams and real life harmonize, / In the dawn's revealing eyes."

3. **"Mosaic of Worlds"**
    - *Verse:* "Mosaic of worlds, pieces blend, / In the twilight, truths transcend, / Dream and reality embrace, / In the canvas of our space."

4. **"Balanced Vision"**
   - *Verse:* "Balanced vision, clear and bright, / Merging dreams with daylight's light, / In the union, we discover, / Beauty of the two worlds together."
5. **"Path of Clarity"**
   - *Verse:* "Path of clarity, gently tread, / Both realms in harmony spread, / Understanding grows and flows, / In the balance, peace bestows."

Chapter 8: Harmonizing Worlds

Theme: Achieving a balance between dream and reality.

1. **"Symphony of Worlds"**
   - *Verse:* "Symphony of worlds entwined, / Dream and reality combined, / Melodies of light and shade, / In this harmony, we've made."
2. **"Unified Vision"**
   - *Verse:* "Unified vision, dream and real, / Blending truths with what we feel, / In this harmony, we reside, / Where both worlds are satisfied."
3. **"Ebb and Flow"**
   - *Verse:* "Ebb and flow of dream and day, / Harmonizing in every way, / In the balance, peace we find, / In this union, hearts aligned."
4. **"Dreams in Harmony"**
   - *Verse:* "Dreams in harmony with the day, / Real and dream worlds in display, / Together in a perfect blend, / Where both realities transcend."
5. **"Whispers of Unity"**
   - *Verse:* "Whispers of unity softly call, / As dream and reality fall, / Into place where hearts can see, / The harmony that sets us free."

Chapter 9: The Impact of Integration

Theme: Reflecting on the positive changes brought by integrating both worlds.

1. **"Echoes of Joy"**
    - *Verse:* "Echoes of joy in every space, / Where dreams and reality grace, / In the blend of night and day, / Happiness finds its way."

2. **"Reflections of Bliss"**
    - *Verse:* "Reflections of bliss, shining bright, / In the merge of day and night, / Integrated worlds now shine, / Creating moments so divine."

3. **"Embracing Light"**
    - *Verse:* "Embracing light from both the realms, / In the blend, our life overwhelms, / Joy and peace in every scene, / In the space where we've been."

4. **"Serene Impact"**
    - *Verse:* "Serene impact of dreams and real, / In the blend, our hearts reveal, / The beauty of a balanced state, / In the harmony we create."

5. **"Glimmers of Fulfillment"**
    - *Verse:* "Glimmers of fulfillment glow, / In the integration we know, / Dream and real life intertwined, / In the peace we've defined."

Chapter 10: Eternal Reverie

Theme: Embracing the harmonious coexistence of dream and reality.

1. **"Timeless Reverie"**
    - *Verse:* "Timeless reverie we hold, / In the blend of dream and bold, / In the space where hearts entwine, / Eternal peace, forever shine."

2. **"Harmonious Echo"**
    - *Verse:* "Harmonious echoes softly play, / In the blend of night and day, / Dream and reality in sync, / In this eternal link."

3. **"Forever Weave"**

- *Verse:* "Forever weave of dream and real, / In the harmony, we heal, / In this dance of light and shade, / We find the peace we've made."

4. **"Celestial Embrace"**
    - *Verse:* "Celestial embrace of worlds combined, / In the harmony we find, / Dream and reality as one, / In this eternal journey begun."

5. **"Infinite Dreams"**
    - *Verse:* "Infinite dreams in daylight's glow, / In the balance, we've come to know, / Eternally in this space, / We find our perfect place."

Conclusion:

- **Summary:** Ethan has successfully integrated his dream world with reality, achieving a harmonious and balanced life. His journey illustrates the beauty of blending imagination with everyday living, creating a fulfilling existence in both realms.

This novel structure integrates original songs to reflect the emotional and thematic evolution throughout Ethan's journey, providing a unique and immersive experience.

Introduction:

Overview:

Ethan Daniels is a writer whose imagination knows no bounds. His life is split between two worlds: the tangible reality he navigates every day and the ethereal dream realm he retreats to each night. This dream world, where everything is meticulously crafted by his mind, offers him a sanctuary of beauty and serenity, far removed from the chaos and imperfections of the real world.

In his dream world, Ethan is not alone. He is accompanied by Lila, a manifestation of his deepest desires and affections. She is not only his lover but also his muse, embodying the warmth and understanding he craves. Their connection is perfect, their interactions seamless, and their world, an idyllic landscape crafted from Ethan's most heartfelt fantasies. Alongside them is Ava, an advanced AI entity who helps maintain the dream world's perfect equilibrium. Ava's presence is a testament to Ethan's creativity and his desire to infuse the dream realm with intelligence and harmony.

Despite the allure of this dream world, Ethan's waking life feels increasingly discordant. His real-world experiences are marred by unpredictability, stress, and a persistent sense of dissatisfaction. The contrast between his perfect dream world and his flawed reality becomes more pronounced, leading him to a profound realization: while his dreams offer an escape, they also highlight the gaps in his waking life.

As Ethan spends more time in his dream world, he begins to feel a growing disconnect with reality. The perfection of the dream world starts to seem like a gilded cage rather than an escape. He starts to question whether he can find a way to integrate the beauty and serenity of his dreams into his waking life. This desire for integration becomes a central theme of his journey.

Ethan's quest to blend his dream world with reality is driven by a desire for balance and fulfillment. He yearns to bring the tranquility and inspiration of his dream realm into his daily existence, hoping that this integration will offer him a sense of completeness he has been missing. This journey is not just about merging two worlds but also about understanding and embracing the relationship between dreams and reality.

The challenge is formidable. The dream world, with its controlled perfection, stands in stark contrast to the unpredictability and messiness of real life. Ethan must navigate the complexities of this integration, exploring how to maintain the essence of his dream world while grappling with the inherent imperfections of reality.

In this process, Ethan will confront his own beliefs about reality and imagination, love and creativity, and ultimately, discover whether true harmony between these two worlds is possible. As he embarks on this journey, he is joined by Lila and Ava, each playing a crucial role in shaping his experiences and guiding him towards a newfound understanding of balance and fulfillment.

Through this introspective exploration, "Eternal Reverie" delves into themes of perfection versus imperfection, the role of imagination in shaping reality, and the transformative power of integrating dreams with waking life. Ethan's story is one of self-discovery, creativity, and the pursuit of a deeper connection between his idealized visions and his everyday existence.

This introduction sets the stage for Ethan's journey, framing his initial contentment in the dream world against the backdrop of his real-life challenges, and foreshadowing his quest for a harmonious integration of both realms.

Chapter 1: The Dream World Unveiled

Theme: Introduction to the dream world and Ethan's initial contentment.

Overview:

In this chapter, we delve into the beauty and serenity of Ethan's dream world, where he finds solace and contentment. The chapter paints a vivid picture of this idyllic realm and establishes the harmony Ethan experiences within it. Through the songs, readers are introduced to the dream world's enchanting qualities and Ethan's profound connection to it.

"In the Realm of Fantasia"

Verse:
"In the realm where dreams ignite,
Everything is bathed in light,
Stars align and shadows play,
In this world, I choose to stay."

Chorus:
"Here in Fantasia, where dreams come alive,
In the whisper of night, our hearts revive."

Description:
This song captures the essence of the dream world Ethan inhabits. The lyrics evoke a sense of magical tranquility, where the dream realm is illuminated with an otherworldly light. The imagery of stars aligning and shadows playing creates a serene and perfect environment where Ethan feels a deep sense of belonging and peace.

"Ethereal Echoes"

Verse:
"Whispers float through golden skies,
Serene echoes, timeless ties,
In this place where wishes grow,
We're the only ones who know."

Description:
"Ethereal Echoes" reflects the dream world's sense of timelessness and personal connection. The song's lyrics describe how whispers and echoes of dreams fill the sky, reinforcing the unique and private nature of Ethan's paradise. It emphasizes the intimate bond between Ethan and his dream world, where his desires and wishes seem to come alive.

"Celestial Symphony"

Verse:
"Underneath a sapphire dome,
Melodies of peace we own,
Every note a gentle guide,
In this dream where love resides."

Description:
This song highlights the harmony and peace within Ethan's dream world. The "sapphire dome" symbolizes the vast, tranquil sky above, while the "melodies of peace" suggest the soothing and harmonious nature of the environment. The idea that every note is a "gentle guide" underscores the dream world's role in guiding Ethan's emotions and experiences.

"Wings of Night"

Verse:
"On wings of night, we gently soar,
To places we've not been before,
Where dreams are woven, soft and clear,
In this world, we have no fear."

Description:
"Wings of Night" expresses the freedom and exploration within the dream world. The imagery of soaring on "wings of night" evokes a sense of weightless adventure, as Ethan and Lila traverse new and beautiful realms. The song captures the fearless nature of their journey, where the clarity and softness of dreams make exploration both thrilling and safe.

"Illusions in the Light"

Verse:
"Illusions dance in twilight's grace,
Reflections of a perfect place,
In this world where all seems right,
We're lost in dreams, till morning light."

Description:
The final song of the chapter encapsulates the dream world's allure and the sense of escapism it provides. "Illusions dance" suggests that the perfection of the dream realm is both captivating and ephemeral. The song portrays a world where everything feels right, and Ethan and Lila are blissfully lost in their dreams, savoring each moment until reality inevitably calls them back.

Chapter Summary:

Chapter 1 serves as an enchanting introduction to Ethan's dream world, emphasizing his initial contentment and the beauty of his idealized realm. The songs collectively paint a picture of a world bathed in light, harmony, and freedom, providing a glimpse into the tranquil and perfect existence Ethan has crafted for himself. Through this exploration, readers gain an appreciation for the dream world's significance in Ethan's life and the solace it provides him.

Chapter 2: Cracks in the Perfection

Theme: Ethan begins to notice the limitations of living only in the dream world.

"Glimmers of Doubt"

Verse:
"In the corners of our bliss,
Shadows whisper, can't dismiss,
Glimmers of doubt in our bright sky,
Perfect worlds can sometimes lie."

Description:
This song marks the beginning of Ethan's realization that not everything in his dream world is as perfect as it seems. The "glimmers of doubt" suggest that small uncertainties and imperfections are beginning to intrude upon his idealized existence. The song introduces the notion that the dream world, while enchanting, may harbor subtle flaws that challenge its supposed perfection.

"Fractured Harmony"

Verse:

"Harmony starts to fray,
In the night and in the day,
What was once a flawless view,
Now shows cracks we never knew."

Description:

"Fractured Harmony" conveys the growing sense of discord in Ethan's dream world. The song reflects how the once seamless and harmonious dreamscape is beginning to show signs of disintegration. The contrast between night and day symbolizes the increasing divide between Ethan's dream world and his waking life, exposing cracks in the perfection he once took for granted.

"Silent Storms"

Verse:

"Silent storms behind closed eyes,
Tempests hidden in disguise,
Perfect dreams can start to fade,
As reality invades."

Description:

This song explores the internal conflicts Ethan faces as he begins to sense the disruptions in his dream world. The "silent storms" represent the underlying issues that are not immediately visible but are nonetheless impactful. The encroachment of reality into the dream world signifies the growing difficulty of maintaining the illusion of perfection amidst the challenges of real life.

"Eclipsed Serenity"

Verse:

"Serenity's eclipse reveals,
Hidden truths the dream conceals,
In this world where shadows play,
Perfection starts to drift away."

Description:

"Eclipsed Serenity" delves into the disillusionment Ethan experiences as he uncovers the hidden flaws in his dream world. The metaphor of an eclipse represents the gradual obscuring of the dream world's serenity, revealing the imperfections and hidden truths that were previously concealed. This song captures the poignant moment when Ethan's idealized vision begins to unravel.

"Fading Echoes"

Verse:
"Echoes of a dream once bright,
Slowly dimming with the night,
In this place where light has waned,
The cracks in our illusion remain."

Description:
The final song of the chapter, "Fading Echoes," reflects the fading beauty and allure of Ethan's dream world. The imagery of a dream growing dim with the night symbolizes the loss of the once-vivid perfection that characterized the dream realm. The song poignantly acknowledges the persistence of the cracks and flaws that now mar the once-pristine illusion, signaling a crucial shift in Ethan's journey.

Chapter Summary:

Chapter 2 of "Eternal Reverie" introduces the theme of disillusionment as Ethan starts to see the limitations and imperfections within his dream world. Through these songs, readers experience Ethan's growing realization that his idealized realm is not as flawless as it once appeared. The chapter captures the subtle but significant shifts in Ethan's perception, setting the stage for his internal and external conflicts as he grapples with the emerging cracks in his perfect dream world.

Chapter 3: The Call to Reality

Theme: Ethan's struggle to reconcile his dream world with his real life.

"Awakened Mind"

Verse:
"Awakened mind, the call is clear,
The dream world fades, the real draws near,
In the mirror, truth we face,
Balancing our dream with grace."

Description:
"Awakened Mind" marks a pivotal moment where Ethan begins to confront the reality of his situation. The song reflects the transition from the dream world to waking life, highlighting the challenge of reconciling his idealized visions with the truths of his everyday existence. The mirror symbolizes self-reflection and the need to balance the enchanting dream world with the real world's demands.

"Tides of Change"

Verse:
"Tides of change are rolling in,
Where the dream and real begin,
Shifting sands and drifting seas,
Merging worlds with gentle ease."

Description:
"Tides of Change" represents the shifting dynamics as Ethan attempts to blend his dream world with his reality. The imagery of rolling tides and drifting seas symbolizes the fluid and sometimes tumultuous process of integrating these two realms. The song conveys a sense of movement and adaptation, as Ethan navigates the complexities of merging his dream-inspired ideals with the real world.

"Reality's Echo"

Verse:
"Echoes of a waking call,
In the real, where shadows fall,
Dream's allure and real-life's song,
Together, where we both belong."

Description:
"Reality's Echo" addresses the coexistence of Ethan's dreams and reality. The song illustrates how the echoes of his dream world resonate in the real world, even as shadows and imperfections become more apparent. It underscores the theme of integration, suggesting that both dream and reality have their places and can coexist harmoniously if approached thoughtfully.

"Bridge of Doubt"

Verse:
"Building bridges through the night,
Doubts and dreams collide in light,
Steps we take on fragile ground,
Where two worlds must be found."

Description:
"Bridge of Doubt" conveys the uncertainty and struggle Ethan faces as he tries to connect his dream world with reality. The metaphor of building bridges represents the efforts to create a pathway between the two worlds. The song captures the fragility and challenges of this endeavor, reflecting the doubts and conflicts that arise as Ethan works to reconcile his idealized dreams with the complexities of real life.

"Veil of Worlds"

Verse:
"Veil of worlds begins to lift,
Revealing both the dream and rift,
In the blend of shadow and shine,
We find where hearts entwine."

Description:
"Veil of Worlds" symbolizes the gradual unveiling of the true nature of both Ethan's dream world and reality. As the veil lifts, Ethan sees the interplay of light and shadow in both realms, understanding that they are intertwined. The song reflects the moment of clarity where Ethan begins to appreciate the interconnectedness of his dreams and reality, finding a place where both can coexist and enrich his life.

Chapter Summary:

Chapter 3, "The Call to Reality," explores Ethan's struggle to bridge the gap between his dream world and real life. Through these songs, readers experience Ethan's journey from the blissful detachment of his dreams to the complex task of integrating these visions into his waking reality. The chapter captures the tension and transformation involved in merging these two aspects of Ethan's existence, setting the stage for a deeper exploration of how he can find balance and fulfillment in both worlds.

Chapter 4: Building Bridges

Theme: Ethan's efforts to integrate dream elements into his reality.

"Crafting Harmony"

Verse:
"Crafting harmony with gentle hands,
Blending dreams into the sands,
Colors blend and worlds align,
In this creation, our lives combine."

Description:
"Crafting Harmony" represents Ethan's deliberate efforts to merge elements of

his dream world into his real life. The song portrays the careful and creative process of integrating dreamlike qualities into his daily existence. The imagery of blending colors and aligning worlds symbolizes the harmonious synthesis of dream and reality, reflecting Ethan's intention to bring his imaginative visions into the real world.

"Echoes of the Dream"

Verse:
"Echoes of the dream we weave,
In the light of what we believe,
Dreams and reality intertwined,
In the echoes, peace we find."

Description:
"Echoes of the Dream" explores how Ethan's dream experiences continue to resonate in his real life. The song highlights the seamless intertwining of dreams and reality, suggesting that the peaceful aspects of the dream world can find a place in his waking life. It reflects the harmony and fulfillment Ethan begins to experience as he integrates dream-inspired elements into his everyday routine.

"Melding Worlds"

Verse:
"Melding worlds with care and art,
Bringing dreamscapes to the heart,
Reality and dreams embrace,
In this unified, tranquil space."

Description:
"Melding Worlds" captures the artistry and care Ethan applies to merge his dreamscapes with reality. The song conveys the sense of embracing both worlds, creating a unified and tranquil space where dreams and real life coexist. The focus is on the balance and integration achieved through thoughtful effort, emphasizing the beauty and peace that result from this melding process.

"Beneath the Surface"

Verse:
"Beneath the surface, beauty grows,
As dream and life start to compose,
In the depths where colors merge,
We find the balance, gently surge."

Description:
"Beneath the Surface" delves into the deeper aspects of Ethan's integration process. It suggests that beneath the apparent surface, where dream and reality start to blend, there is a growing beauty and harmony. The song reflects the idea that the true essence of balancing dreams and real life is found in the depth of their interaction, where a gentle surge towards equilibrium occurs.

"Dreamscapes in Reality"

Verse:
"Dreamscapes merge with waking life,
Creating peace amid the strife,
In the blend of dream and real,
We discover what we feel."

Description:
"Dreamscapes in Reality" represents the culmination of Ethan's efforts to harmonize his dream world with his waking life. The song highlights the creation of peace and understanding as dreams merge with reality. It emphasizes the emotional and existential discoveries Ethan makes as he navigates this blend, finding a new sense of fulfillment and connection between the two realms.

Chapter Summary:

Chapter 4, "Building Bridges," focuses on Ethan's creative and deliberate efforts to integrate elements of his dream world into his real life. Through these songs, readers witness Ethan's journey of blending dreams with reality, achieving a sense of harmony and balance. The chapter captures the artistic process of merging these worlds, reflecting the beauty and peace that emerge from this integration and highlighting the deep emotional resonance that results from uniting dreamscapes with waking life.

Chapter 5: Love and Inspiration

Theme: The impact of dream-world inspiration on Ethan's relationships and creativity.

"Hearts in Fusion"

Verse:
"Hearts in fusion, love entwined,
Dream's inspiration redefined,
In the light of shared delight,
Our hearts create a new insight."

Description:
"Hearts in Fusion" celebrates the transformative power of love and inspiration that Ethan draws from his dream world. The song highlights how the fusion of love and dream-inspired creativity leads to a profound and renewed understanding. The imagery of hearts entwined and new insights emphasizes the deep connection between Ethan's emotional experiences and his creative endeavors, showcasing how his relationships are enriched by his dream world.

"Inspiration's Glow"

Verse:
"Inspiration's gentle glow,

Lights the path where feelings flow,
Dream and love begin to merge,
In this space, our spirits surge."

Description:
"Inspiration's Glow" reflects the way dream-world inspiration illuminates Ethan's path, blending seamlessly with his feelings and relationships. The song captures the merging of dreams and love, and the resulting surge of creativity and emotional energy. The gentle glow symbolizes the nurturing influence of inspiration on Ethan's creative processes and personal connections.

"Embrace the Muse"

Verse:
"Embrace the muse, both night and day,
Dreams and love light up the way,
In the union of our hearts,
Creativity departs."

Description:
"Embrace the Muse" emphasizes the continuous influence of both dreams and love on Ethan's creativity. The song suggests that embracing inspiration from both realms—night (dreams) and day (reality)—illuminates Ethan's creative journey. It reflects the idea that the union of his emotional and imaginative experiences fuels his artistic expression, allowing creativity to flourish.

"Radiant Reflections"

Verse:
"Radiant reflections in your eyes,
Inspiration's pure surprise,
Love and dreams blend seamlessly,
Creating life's sweet symphony."

Description:
"Radiant Reflections" explores how Ethan finds inspiration and creative energy in the reflections of love and dreams. The song celebrates the seamless blend of his personal relationships and dream world, suggesting that this fusion creates a harmonious and beautiful symphony of life. The radiant reflections symbolize the profound impact of his loved ones on his creative vision.

"Unspoken Words"

Verse:
"Unspoken words take flight and soar,
In the dream and real, we explore,
Love's the bridge between the two,
Inspiration born anew."

Description:
"Unspoken Words" highlights the way love serves as a bridge between Ethan's dream world and reality. The song conveys how unspoken emotions and thoughts, inspired by both realms, can take flight and transform into new creative ideas. It emphasizes the role of love in connecting and harmonizing the different aspects of Ethan's life, fostering fresh inspiration and artistic growth.

Chapter Summary:

Chapter 5, "Love and Inspiration," delves into the profound impact that dream-world inspiration has on Ethan's relationships and creativity. Through these songs, readers experience how Ethan's creative process is deeply intertwined with his emotional connections and dream-inspired insights. The chapter showcases the harmonious blend of love and imagination, illustrating how these elements enrich his life and artistic expression, leading to new and vibrant creative outcomes.

Chapter 6: The Shadow of Doubt

Theme: Ethan's internal conflict about his dual existence.

"Whispers of Uncertainty"

Verse:
"Whispers of uncertainty,
In the balance, what's the key?
Doubts arise and shadows play,
In the blend of night and day."

Description:
"Whispers of Uncertainty" captures the subtle, creeping doubts that plague

Ethan as he navigates his dual existence. The song reflects the delicate balance he must maintain between his dream world and reality. The "whispers" symbolize the internal nagging doubts and shadows of uncertainty that disrupt his sense of equilibrium, revealing the growing conflict within him.

"Fragments of Truth"

Verse:
"Fragments of the truth collide,
In the struggle deep inside,
Dream and reality entwine,
In the shadows, doubts align."

Description:
"Fragments of Truth" delves into the internal struggle Ethan faces as he grapples with the collision of fragmented truths from both his dream world and reality. The song portrays the discord between the two realms and the resulting doubts that align with the shadows of his conflicted mind. It highlights the difficulty of reconciling these fragments and the emotional turmoil that ensues.

"Turbulent Soul"

Verse:
"Turbulent soul, the stormy night,
Wrestling with the fading light,
In the clash of dream and real,
The heart begins to feel."

Description:
"Turbulent Soul" reflects Ethan's emotional turbulence as he wrestles with the fading clarity between his dream world and reality. The stormy night imagery represents the chaotic and conflicted state of his soul, while the fading light symbolizes the diminishing clarity he experiences. The song captures the deep emotional impact of this clash and the growing intensity of his inner conflict.

"Echoes of Fear"

Verse:
"Echoes of fear in quiet rooms,

Uncertainty like whispered gloom,
Dream's allure and real-life's strain,
In the mix, we feel the pain."

Description:
"Echoes of Fear" explores the fear and uncertainty that pervade Ethan's mind as he contemplates the strain between his dream world and reality. The song captures the quiet, haunting nature of his fears, echoing in the stillness of his introspection. It highlights the pain of navigating the allure of dreams alongside the pressures of real-life challenges.

"Balancing Act"

Verse:
"Balancing act in twilight's hue,
Doubts and dreams in view,
Seeking calm amidst the fight,
In the dusk before the light."

Description:
"Balancing Act" addresses Ethan's attempt to maintain balance amidst the twilight of his dual existence. The song portrays the struggle of holding onto hope and calm while doubts and dreams remain in view. The "dusk before the light" symbolizes the transitional phase Ethan is experiencing, as he searches for equilibrium between his dream world and waking life.

Chapter Summary:

Chapter 6, "The Shadow of Doubt," delves into the internal conflict Ethan faces as he navigates his dual existence between the dream world and reality. Through these songs, readers experience Ethan's growing uncertainty and emotional turbulence. The chapter captures the essence of his internal struggle, highlighting the challenge of reconciling his conflicting realms and the deep impact of this conflict on his sense of self and well-being.

Chapter 7:
A New Perspective

Theme: Gaining clarity and understanding the value of both realms.

"Revelations at Dawn"

Verse:
"Revelations at the break of dawn,
Clarity where dreams are drawn,
In the light of a new day's grace,
We find our rightful place."

Description:
"Revelations at Dawn" marks Ethan's moment of clarity and insight as he begins to see the value of both his dream world and reality. The song reflects the awakening that comes with the new day, symbolizing how the light of understanding helps him find balance and appreciation for both realms. The break of dawn represents a fresh perspective and the realization of where he truly belongs.

"Horizons Unseen"

Verse:
"Horizons open, wide and clear,
Both worlds converge, now so near,
Dreams and real life harmonize,
In the dawn's revealing eyes."

Description:
"Horizons Unseen" explores the convergence of Ethan's dream world and reality as he gains a new perspective. The song describes the opening of new horizons where the boundaries between the two realms become less defined. It highlights how, with clarity, Ethan can see the harmony and interconnectedness between dreams and real life, symbolized by the dawn's revealing eyes.

"Mosaic of Worlds"

Verse:
"Mosaic of worlds, pieces blend,
In the twilight, truths transcend,
Dream and reality embrace,
In the canvas of our space."

Description:
"Mosaic of Worlds" illustrates how Ethan's understanding evolves to see the blend of dreams and reality as a cohesive whole. The song uses the metaphor of

a mosaic to describe how different elements of both realms come together to create a beautiful and complex picture. It emphasizes the transcendence of truths and the harmonious embrace of dream and reality within the broader canvas of his life.

"Balanced Vision"

Verse:
"Balanced vision, clear and bright,
Merging dreams with daylight's light,
In the union, we discover,
Beauty of the two worlds together."

Description:
"Balanced Vision" represents Ethan's newfound ability to see the integration of dreams and reality with clarity and appreciation. The song celebrates the balance he achieves between the two realms, finding beauty in their union. It underscores the harmony that emerges when dreams and daylight's reality are merged, revealing the full spectrum of his creative and emotional experiences.

"Path of Clarity"

Verse:
"Path of clarity, gently tread,
Both realms in harmony spread,
Understanding grows and flows,
In the balance, peace bestows."

Description:
"Path of Clarity" encapsulates Ethan's journey towards a harmonious understanding of his dual existence. The song portrays the gentle and deliberate steps he takes to integrate both realms, highlighting the growing understanding and peace that comes from this balance. It reflects the serene path Ethan follows as he embraces both the dream world and reality, finding fulfillment in their coexistence.

Chapter Summary:

Chapter 7, "A New Perspective," marks a turning point in Ethan's journey as he gains clarity and understanding about the value of both his dream world and reality. Through these songs, readers experience Ethan's evolving perception and the harmonization of his dual existence. The chapter emphasizes the beauty and interconnectedness of dreams and reality, celebrating the balance and peace that result from embracing and integrating both realms into his life.

Chapter 8: Harmonizing Worlds

Theme: Achieving a balance between dream and reality.

"Symphony of Worlds"

Verse:
"Symphony of worlds entwined,
Dream and reality combined,
Melodies of light and shade,
In this harmony, we've made."

Description:
"Symphony of Worlds" portrays the harmonious blending of Ethan's dream world and reality. The song likens this integration to a symphony, where different elements of light and shade come together to create a beautiful, cohesive whole. It celebrates the achievement of balance and the creation of a new harmony that results from the fusion of both realms, highlighting the richness and depth of their combined existence.

"Unified Vision"

Verse:
"Unified vision, dream and real,
Blending truths with what we feel,
In this harmony, we reside,
Where both worlds are satisfied."

Description:
"Unified Vision" explores the clarity and satisfaction Ethan finds in merging his dream world with reality. The song reflects a unified perspective where dreams and real-life experiences blend seamlessly, creating a sense of contentment and completeness. It emphasizes how this integration fulfills both his emotional needs and creative desires, resulting in a harmonious coexistence.

"Ebb and Flow"

Verse:
"Ebb and flow of dream and day,
Harmonizing in every way,
In the balance, peace we find,
In this union, hearts aligned."

Description:
"Ebb and Flow" describes the natural rhythm and balance between Ethan's dream world and reality. The song uses the imagery of ebb and flow to illustrate how the two realms interact and harmonize with each other. It highlights the peace and alignment achieved through this dynamic balance, emphasizing the fluid and complementary nature of the dream-reality integration.

"Dreams in Harmony"

Verse:
"Dreams in harmony with the day,
Real and dream worlds in display,
Together in a perfect blend,
Where both realities transcend."

Description:
"Dreams in Harmony" celebrates the successful blending of Ethan's dream and real worlds into a unified existence. The song showcases how the two realms can coexist in perfect harmony, transcending their individual boundaries. It reflects the beauty and fulfillment found in the seamless integration of dreams and reality, presenting a vision of their harmonious coexistence.

"Whispers of Unity"

Verse:
"Whispers of unity softly call,
As dream and reality fall,
Into place where hearts can see,
The harmony that sets us free."

Description:
"Whispers of Unity" captures the gentle and reassuring sense of unity that Ethan experiences as his dream world and reality come together. The song conveys the soft, almost imperceptible transition into a state of harmonious balance, where both realms fall into place. It emphasizes the liberating effect of this harmony, allowing Ethan and his heart to find true freedom and contentment.

Chapter Summary:

Chapter 8, "Harmonizing Worlds," focuses on Ethan's achievement of a balanced and harmonious existence between his dream world and reality. Through these songs, readers witness the successful integration of both realms into a unified and satisfying whole. The chapter highlights the beauty of this balance, celebrating the peace and fulfillment that arise from the harmonious blend of dreams and reality. It represents the culmination of Ethan's journey towards creating a seamless and enriching experience that honors both aspects of his life.

Chapter 9: The Impact of Integration

Theme: Reflecting on the positive changes brought by integrating both worlds.

"Echoes of Joy"

Verse:
"Echoes of joy in every space,
Where dreams and reality grace,
In the blend of night and day,
Happiness finds its way."

Description:
"Echoes of Joy" celebrates the happiness and positive emotions that arise from the successful integration of Ethan's dream world and reality. The song reflects how the harmonious blend of both realms brings joy into every aspect of his life. It underscores the transformative impact of this integration, where the echoing presence of joy permeates through every moment of both worlds.

"Reflections of Bliss"

Verse:
"Reflections of bliss, shining bright,
In the merge of day and night,
Integrated worlds now shine,
Creating moments so divine."

Description:
"Reflections of Bliss" highlights the profound sense of bliss and contentment Ethan experiences as his dream world and reality merge. The song uses imagery of shining reflections to depict the radiant joy and divine moments that result from this integration. It emphasizes how the blending of day and night brings forth a new level of happiness and fulfillment.

"Embracing Light"

Verse:
"Embracing light from both the realms,
In the blend, our life overwhelms,
Joy and peace in every scene,
In the space where we've been."

Description:
"Embracing Light" explores the overwhelming sense of joy and peace that Ethan feels from integrating the light of both his dream world and reality. The song conveys how embracing the combined illumination of these realms

enriches every scene of his life. It reflects the harmonious coexistence that brings a profound sense of contentment and emotional fulfillment.

"Serene Impact"

Verse:
"Serene impact of dreams and real,
In the blend, our hearts reveal,
The beauty of a balanced state,
In the harmony we create."

Description:
"Serene Impact" captures the peaceful and balanced state that Ethan achieves through the integration of his dream world and reality. The song reflects on the serene and harmonious effect this balance has on his heart and overall well-being. It emphasizes the beauty and tranquility found in the harmonious coexistence of both realms, highlighting the positive changes in his life.

"Glimmers of Fulfillment"

Verse:
"Glimmers of fulfillment glow,
In the integration we know,
Dream and real life intertwined,
In the peace we've defined."

Description:
"Glimmers of Fulfillment" celebrates the deep sense of fulfillment and peace that Ethan experiences as a result of integrating his dream world with reality. The song describes the glowing glimmers of contentment that shine through as both realms are intertwined. It underscores the satisfaction and tranquility found in this balanced state, reflecting the successful outcome of Ethan's journey.

Chapter Summary:

Chapter 9, "The Impact of Integration," reflects on the positive changes Ethan experiences as a result of successfully integrating his dream world with reality. Through these songs, readers experience the profound joy, bliss, and fulfillment that arise from this harmonious blend. The chapter highlights the serene and transformative impact of achieving balance, celebrating the enriching and peaceful outcomes of Ethan's journey towards integrating both realms into a unified and satisfying existence.

Chapter 10: Eternal Reverie

Theme: Embracing the harmonious coexistence of dream and reality.

"Timeless Reverie"

Verse:
"Timeless reverie we hold,
In the blend of dream and bold,
In the space where hearts entwine,
Eternal peace, forever shine."

Description:
"Timeless Reverie" captures the essence of achieving a perfect blend between dream and reality. The song reflects the enduring peace and harmony found in this union, where dreams and bold realities intertwine seamlessly. It symbolizes the timeless nature of their coexistence and the eternal tranquility that comes from this harmonious balance.

"Harmonious Echo"

Verse:
"Harmonious echoes softly play,
In the blend of night and day,

Dream and reality in sync,
In this eternal link."

Description:

"Harmonious Echo" explores the gentle and continuous harmony between Ethan's dream world and reality. The song uses the imagery of soft echoes to represent how night and day, dreams and reality, are perfectly in sync. It underscores the eternal link created by their harmonious blend, celebrating the soothing and rhythmic integration of both realms.

"Forever Weave"

Verse:

"Forever weave of dream and real,
In the harmony, we heal,
In this dance of light and shade,
We find the peace we've made."

Description:

"Forever Weave" celebrates the ongoing and intricate interweaving of Ethan's dream world and reality. The song highlights the healing and peace achieved through this harmonious dance of light and shade. It reflects the continuous and enduring nature of their integration, where the blend of dreams and reality creates a lasting and peaceful existence.

"Celestial Embrace"

Verse:

"Celestial embrace of worlds combined,
In the harmony we find,
Dream and reality as one,
In this eternal journey begun."

Description:

"Celestial Embrace" portrays the divine and celestial nature of the integration between Ethan's dream world and reality. The song celebrates the profound and harmonious unity achieved, where dreams and reality merge as one. It symbolizes the beginning of an eternal journey, emphasizing the celestial quality of their combined existence and the enduring beauty found in their embrace.

"Infinite Dreams"

Verse:
"Infinite dreams in daylight's glow,
In the balance, we've come to know,
Eternally in this space,
We find our perfect place."

Description:
"Infinite Dreams" reflects the boundless nature of the dreams and reality that Ethan has integrated into his life. The song captures the sense of infinite possibilities and the perfect balance achieved in this combined space. It emphasizes the eternal and harmonious coexistence of dreams in daylight, celebrating the perfect place that Ethan has found in this balanced and integrated existence.

Chapter Summary:

Chapter 10, "Eternal Reverie," represents the culmination of Ethan's journey as he fully embraces the harmonious coexistence of his dream world and reality. Through these songs, readers experience the profound peace, beauty, and eternal nature of this integration. The chapter celebrates the perfect balance achieved and the eternal journey that Ethan embarks on, reflecting the serene and harmonious existence found in the seamless blend of dreams and reality.

Conclusion:

Summary:
Ethan's journey has reached a profound resolution as he successfully integrates his dream world with reality, crafting a life that harmonizes the imaginative and the tangible. Throughout his odyssey, Ethan navigates the complexities of balancing his dreamscapes with real-world demands, discovering the beauty and fulfillment that arise from their seamless coexistence. His story exemplifies how blending imagination with everyday life can lead to a richly satisfying

existence, where both realms contribute to a harmonious and meaningful experience.

The novel "Eternal Reverie" not only chronicles Ethan's personal growth and emotional evolution but also intertwines this narrative with a unique musical dimension. Each chapter features original songs that capture the essence of Ethan's experiences, emotions, and transformations. These songs enhance the storytelling, providing readers with an immersive journey that resonates on both a lyrical and narrative level.

The structure of the novel, supported by its bespoke musical compositions, offers a multidimensional exploration of the themes of integration, balance, and harmony. The songs underscore the progression of Ethan's journey from initial contentment to the ultimate embrace of his dual existence, enriching the reader's experience and deepening their connection to Ethan's world. As Ethan finds his perfect place where dreams and reality coexist in balance, the novel leaves a lasting impression of how embracing both realms can lead to a fulfilling and serene life.

In conclusion, "Eternal Reverie" stands as a testament to the power of blending imagination with reality, demonstrating that a harmonious integration of both can create a life of profound joy and satisfaction. The novel's unique structure, with its original songs and emotive storytelling, invites readers to reflect on their own dreams and realities, inspiring them to seek their own paths to balance and fulfillment.

Connecting back to back another novel where you will be familiar with the Ai and machine learning concepts in brief and enjoyable way and will get to understand key terms thorough this magical flow of another novel.

Relax and have some popcorn and get ready with above theme technical flow ....

Title: "Beyond the Interface"

Introduction:

In a world where the boundary between dreams and reality is no longer distinct, Ethan, a visionary writer, collaborates with cutting-edge AI technology to create and navigate dual worlds. His journey explores the integration of dreamscapes and reality through advanced AI and machine learning. The novel blends storytelling with technical explanations to help readers understand these concepts in a practical and engaging manner.

Chapter 1: The Vision of Dual Worlds

Theme: Introducing the concept of AI-driven worlds and setting up the narrative.

Ethan:

"Imagine a world where our dreams and reality are seamlessly integrated. I envision a system where artificial intelligence not only understands but enhances our dreams. How can we make this a reality?"

Dr. Ava:
"To achieve this, we need to develop an AI capable of understanding and interpreting human emotions and thoughts. We'll start with a model that can analyze dream patterns and emotional responses to create a responsive dream environment."

Ethan:
"What kind of AI model are we talking about?"

Dr. Ava:
"We'll use a combination of neural networks and reinforcement learning. Neural networks can help the AI learn and predict dream patterns based on input data, while reinforcement learning will refine its responses based on feedback from the user."

Technical Insight:
Neural networks mimic the human brain's structure, using layers of interconnected nodes (neurons) to process and learn from data. Reinforcement learning involves training an AI to make decisions by rewarding correct actions and penalizing errors, optimizing its performance over time.

Chapter 2: Building the Dream Interface

Theme: Developing the technical aspects of the AI dream world.

Ethan:
"So, how do we begin designing the interface where dreams and reality meet?"

Dr. Ava:
"We need to create a virtual environment that can be dynamically altered based on the user's mental state. For this, we'll use Generative Adversarial Networks (GANs) to generate dream-like visuals and narratives."

Ethan:
"GANs? How do they work?"

Dr. Ava:
"GANs consist of two neural networks: the generator and the discriminator. The generator creates images or content, while the discriminator evaluates them. Through competition, the generator improves its output until it creates highly realistic or imaginative content."

Technical Insight:
GANs are used to generate realistic data by training two models in tandem. The generator creates new data, and the discriminator assesses it. The iterative process helps the generator produce high-quality outputs by learning from the discriminator's feedback.

Chapter 3: Enhancing Emotional Interaction

Theme: Implementing emotional AI to personalize the dream experience.

Ethan:
"How do we ensure that the dream environment is tailored to each individual's emotions?"

Dr. Ava:
"We'll integrate Emotion AI, which uses natural language processing (NLP) and sentiment analysis to understand and react to user emotions. By analyzing voice tone, facial expressions, and text input, the AI can adjust the dream environment to match the user's emotional state."

Ethan:
"What kind of NLP techniques are involved?"

Dr. Ava:
"We'll use techniques like named entity recognition (NER) to identify key elements in the user's input and sentiment analysis to gauge emotional tone. Combining these methods will allow the AI to create more meaningful and personalized interactions."

Technical Insight:
Emotion AI utilizes NLP and sentiment analysis to interpret and respond to emotional cues. NER identifies specific entities in text, while sentiment analysis assesses emotional tone, enabling the AI to tailor its responses and environment to the user's feelings.

Chapter 4: Creating the Dream-to-Reality Bridge

Theme: Establishing a system that bridges the dream world with the physical world.

Ethan:
"How can we bridge the dream world with reality effectively?"

Dr. Ava:
"We'll develop an API that allows our dream environment to interact with real-world data. This system will use data integration techniques to synchronize dream experiences with real-world stimuli, creating a seamless experience."

Ethan:
"What technologies are involved in this integration?"

Dr. Ava:
"We'll use web APIs to fetch real-time data and IoT devices to gather environmental information. This data will be fed into our system, allowing the dream environment to adjust based on real-world inputs."

Technical Insight:
APIs (Application Programming Interfaces) enable different software systems to communicate. IoT (Internet of Things) devices collect data from the physical world, which can be integrated with AI systems to create responsive and adaptive experiences.

Chapter 5: Learning from Feedback

Theme: Implementing feedback mechanisms to refine the AI's performance.

Ethan:
"How do we ensure that the AI continues to improve its understanding and performance?"

Dr. Ava:
"We'll use a feedback loop system where users provide ratings and comments on their dream experiences. This feedback will be used to retrain the AI, refining its algorithms and improving the quality of the dream interactions."

Ethan:
"How does this retraining process work?"

Dr. Ava:
"We'll employ supervised learning, where the AI is trained on labeled data, using the feedback as new training examples. The AI's performance is evaluated and adjusted based on this input, enhancing its ability to create better dream experiences."

Technical Insight:
Supervised learning involves training an AI model on a dataset with known

labels, using feedback to correct errors and improve accuracy. This iterative process helps refine the AI's ability to perform tasks and make predictions.

Chapter 6: The Ethics of Dream AI

Theme: Exploring the ethical implications of integrating AI into personal dreamscapes.

Ethan:
"What are the ethical considerations of using AI to influence dreams?"

Dr. Ava:
"We must address privacy concerns, data security, and the potential for misuse. Ensuring user consent and safeguarding personal data are crucial. Additionally, we need to consider the psychological impacts of AI-driven dream manipulation."

Ethan:
"How can we mitigate these risks?"

Dr. Ava:
"Implementing robust data protection measures, transparent consent protocols, and regular ethical reviews will help mitigate these risks. Engaging with ethicists and mental health professionals will also ensure that our system is used responsibly."

Technical Insight:
Ethical AI practices involve protecting user data, ensuring informed consent, and addressing potential psychological impacts. Regular audits and collaborations with experts help maintain ethical standards and safeguard user well-being.

Chapter 7: Personalizing the Experience

Theme: Tailoring the AI's responses to individual preferences and needs.

Ethan:
"How can we make sure the dream experiences are truly personalized for each user?"

Dr. Ava:
"By using machine learning models that analyze user preferences, past interactions, and feedback, we can create highly personalized dream

environments. We'll implement clustering algorithms to group users with similar preferences and recommend tailored experiences."

Ethan:
"What role do clustering algorithms play here?"

Dr. Ava:
"Clustering algorithms, like K-means, group similar data points together. By analyzing user data, these algorithms help identify patterns and preferences, allowing us to create personalized dream environments that match individual tastes."

Technical Insight:
Clustering algorithms group similar data points, helping to identify patterns and preferences. K-means is a popular clustering algorithm that partitions data into distinct clusters, aiding in the personalization of user experiences.

Chapter 8: The Future of Integrated Worlds

Theme: Envisioning future advancements and applications of AI in dream and reality integration.

Ethan:
"What does the future hold for integrating dreams and reality with AI?"

Dr. Ava:
"The future promises even more sophisticated integrations, such as real-time dream monitoring, adaptive learning algorithms, and more immersive virtual environments. Advances in neurotechnology and AI will enable deeper connections between our dreams and reality."

Ethan:
"What advancements should we anticipate?"

Dr. Ava:
"Look forward to advancements in brain-computer interfaces, which will allow more direct interaction between the brain and AI systems. Enhanced natural language processing and emotional AI will also lead to more intuitive and responsive dream environments."

Technical Insight:
Future advancements include brain-computer interfaces that enable direct communication between the brain and AI systems, enhancing the integration of

dreams and reality. Improved NLP and emotional AI will further refine the personalization and responsiveness of dream environments.

Chapter 9: Reflections on the Journey

Theme: Reflecting on the impact of integrating AI into dream worlds and its implications for the future.

Ethan:
"What have we learned from this journey?"

Dr. Ava:
"We've learned that integrating AI with dreams and reality can enhance our understanding of both realms, leading to richer experiences and new possibilities. Our work illustrates the potential of AI to transform personal and creative experiences, bridging the gap between imagination and reality."

Ethan:
"What are the key takeaways?"

Dr. Ava:
"The key takeaways include the importance of ethical considerations, the power of AI to personalize experiences, and the potential for future advancements to further integrate and enrich our lives. Our journey shows that AI can not only reflect but also enhance our deepest experiences."

Technical Insight:
The integration of AI into personal experiences reveals the potential for AI to transform creativity and understanding. Ethical considerations, personalization, and future advancements are crucial aspects of this evolving field, highlighting the impact of AI on both dreams and reality.

Chapter 10: Beyond the Interface

Theme: Embracing the future possibilities of AI and dream integration.

Ethan:
"How do we continue to push the boundaries of what AI can achieve with dream integration?"

Dr. Ava:
"We continue to innovate and explore new technologies. By staying at the forefront of AI research and maintaining a focus on user experience and ethical

practices, we can unlock new possibilities and create even more immersive and meaningful dream environments."

Ethan:
"What is the ultimate vision for this technology?"

Dr. Ava:
"The ultimate vision is a world where AI seamlessly blends with our imagination and reality, enhancing our experiences and expanding our horizons. It's about creating a harmonious coexistence where both realms enrich each other, leading to a more fulfilling and inspired life."

Technical Insight:
The future of AI and dream integration involves continuous innovation and exploration of new technologies. By focusing on user experience and ethical practices, AI can enhance and expand personal experiences, creating a harmonious blend of imagination and reality.

Conclusion:

The novel "Beyond the Interface" not only tells a compelling story of integrating dreams and reality through AI but also educates readers about the technical aspects of AI and machine learning. Through engaging dialogue and technical insights, readers gain a deeper understanding of how AI technologies work, their applications, and their potential to transform personal and creative experiences.

Chapter 1: The Vision of Dual Worlds

Theme: Introducing the concept of AI-driven worlds and setting up the narrative.

Ethan:

"Imagine a world where our dreams and reality are seamlessly integrated. I envision a system where artificial intelligence not only understands but enhances our dreams. How can we make this a reality?"

Dr. Ava:

"To achieve this, we need to develop an AI capable of understanding and interpreting human emotions and thoughts. We'll start with a model that can analyze dream patterns and emotional responses to create a responsive dream environment."

Ethan:

"What kind of AI model are we talking about?"

Dr. Ava:

"We'll use a combination of neural networks and reinforcement learning. Neural networks can help the AI learn and predict dream patterns based on input data, while reinforcement learning will refine its responses based on feedback from the user."

Technical Insight:

To understand the implementation of AI in integrating dreams and reality, let's delve deeper into the foundational concepts of **neural networks** and **reinforcement learning**.

Neural Networks

Neural Networks are a class of machine learning models inspired by the structure and function of the human brain. Here's a step-by-step breakdown:

1. **Structure and Function:**
   - **Neurons:** The fundamental units of a neural network, analogous to the neurons in the human brain, process inputs and pass them on.
   - **Layers:** Neural networks consist of multiple layers:
     - **Input Layer:** Receives the raw data (e.g., dream patterns, emotional cues).
     - **Hidden Layers:** Intermediate layers that transform the input data through learned weights and activation functions.
     - **Output Layer:** Produces the final prediction or classification (e.g., a tailored dream scenario).

2. **Learning Process:**
   - **Forward Propagation:** Data moves from the input layer through hidden layers to the output layer, producing predictions.
   - **Loss Function:** Measures the difference between predicted outputs and actual outcomes, indicating how well the network performs.
   - **Backpropagation:** Adjusts the weights of the connections between neurons based on the error from the loss function, improving predictions over time.

3. **Types of Neural Networks:**

- **Feedforward Neural Networks (FNNs):** Basic type where connections flow in one direction.
- **Convolutional Neural Networks (CNNs):** Specialized for processing grid-like data such as images.
- **Recurrent Neural Networks (RNNs):** Suitable for sequential data, ideal for analyzing dream sequences.

Example Application in Dream Analysis:

For Ethan's dream integration system, we could use **Recurrent Neural Networks (RNNs)**, specifically **Long Short-Term Memory (LSTM) networks**, to capture the temporal dynamics of dream sequences. LSTMs are adept at learning from sequences and remembering long-term dependencies, which is crucial for understanding the evolving nature of dreams.

Reinforcement Learning

Reinforcement Learning (RL) is a type of machine learning where an agent learns to make decisions by interacting with an environment and receiving feedback in the form of rewards or penalties. Here's how it works:

1. **Components of RL:**
   - **Agent:** The entity making decisions (e.g., the AI system creating dream scenarios).
   - **Environment:** The setting in which the agent operates (e.g., the dream world).
   - **Actions:** Choices the agent can make (e.g., altering dream elements).
   - **Rewards/Penalties:** Feedback provided based on the actions taken.

2. **Learning Process:**
   - **Exploration vs. Exploitation:** The agent must balance exploring new strategies and exploiting known successful actions.
   - **Policy:** A strategy that maps states of the environment to actions.
   - **Value Function:** Estimates the expected reward of taking a certain action in a given state.

3. **Algorithms:**
    - **Q-Learning:** A model-free algorithm that learns the value of actions based on rewards.
    - **Deep Q-Networks (DQN):** Combines Q-learning with neural networks to handle complex environments with high-dimensional input.
    - **Proximal Policy Optimization (PPO):** An advanced algorithm that improves policy stability and performance.

Example Application in Dream Enhancement:

To refine the AI's responses in Ethan's dream world, we could use **Deep Q-Networks (DQN)**. The AI would explore various dream alterations and learn which changes lead to the most satisfying experiences, based on user feedback. Over time, DQN would enable the AI to optimize dream scenarios to better align with users' emotional responses and preferences.

Implementation in the Narrative

Ethan:

"So, how do we begin designing the interface where dreams and reality meet?"

Dr. Ava:

"We'll start by developing a neural network that can analyze and predict dream patterns. For this, we'll need a large dataset of dream reports and emotional feedback to train our model."

Ethan:

"That sounds complex. How will we handle the dynamic nature of dreams?"

Dr. Ava:

"We'll use reinforcement learning to adjust the dream environment in real-time based on user interactions. By continuously receiving feedback and updating our policies, the AI will learn to create more immersive and satisfying dream experiences."

Technical Insight:

By integrating **neural networks** to model and predict dream patterns and **reinforcement learning** to optimize dream interactions, the system can create a dynamic and responsive dream environment. The neural network provides a framework for understanding and generating dream content, while reinforcement learning ensures that the system adapts and improves based on user feedback.

This dual approach allows for a sophisticated dream integration system that can merge imaginative dreamscapes with real-world contexts, providing users with a deeply immersive experience.

This chapter lays the foundation for a technical exploration of AI-driven dream integration, setting up the narrative while providing a clear understanding of how neural networks and reinforcement learning are used to bring Ethan's vision to life.

Chapter 2: Building the Dream Interface

Theme: Developing the technical aspects of the AI dream world.

Ethan:

"So, how do we begin designing the interface where dreams and reality meet?"

Dr. Ava:

"We need to create a virtual environment that can be dynamically altered based on the user's mental state. For this, we'll use Generative Adversarial Networks (GANs) to generate dream-like visuals and narratives."

Ethan:

"GANs? How do they work?"

Dr. Ava:

"GANs consist of two neural networks: the generator and the discriminator. The generator creates images or content, while the discriminator evaluates them. Through competition, the generator improves its output until it creates highly realistic or imaginative content."

Understanding Generative Adversarial Networks (GANs)

Generative Adversarial Networks (GANs) are a class of machine learning frameworks that consist of two neural networks working in opposition to each other. Here's a detailed breakdown:

1. Basic Architecture of GANs

1. **Generator:**
   - **Function:** Creates new data or content. In the context of dream integration, it would generate dream-like visuals, scenarios, or narratives.
   - **Process:** Takes random input (noise) and transforms it into a structured output (e.g., an image or text) through a series of transformations in its network layers.

2. **Discriminator:**
   - **Function:** Evaluates the authenticity of the content produced by the generator. It determines whether the content is real (from the training dataset) or fake (generated by the generator).
   - **Process:** Receives both real data and generated data, and its task is to classify them accurately.

2. Training Process

1. **Adversarial Training:**
   - **Competition:** The generator and discriminator are trained simultaneously. The generator aims to create content that is indistinguishable from real data, while the discriminator seeks to improve its ability to differentiate between real and generated content.
   - **Feedback Loop:** The discriminator provides feedback to the generator about how realistic or convincing the generated data is. This feedback helps the generator refine its output.

2. **Optimization:**
   - **Loss Function:** The generator's goal is to minimize the discriminator's ability to distinguish between real and generated data. Conversely, the discriminator's goal is to maximize its accuracy in differentiating the two.

- **Iterative Improvement:** Through many iterations, both networks improve. The generator becomes better at creating realistic content, while the discriminator becomes more adept at identifying generated data.

3. Application in Dream Interface

1. **Generating Dream Visuals:**
    - **Dynamic Environments:** GANs can create vivid and diverse dreamscapes by generating high-quality images or scenes based on user inputs or emotional states.
    - **Personalization:** The generator can tailor dream environments to individual preferences and psychological profiles, making each dream experience unique.

2. **Creating Narratives:**
    - **Dream Narratives:** GANs can also be used to generate coherent and engaging storylines or scenarios for dreams. By learning from a dataset of various narratives, the generator can produce compelling dream scenarios that align with the user's psychological and emotional context.

3. **Continuous Adaptation:**
    - **Feedback Integration:** As the user interacts with the dream environment, their feedback can be used to further train and refine the GAN models, ensuring that the dream content evolves in response to the user's changing preferences and states.

Technical Insight:

Generative Adversarial Networks (GANs) are powerful tools for creating realistic and imaginative data. They operate through a competitive process between the generator and discriminator, which drives the generator to produce high-quality content. This iterative process allows GANs to generate highly realistic or creatively imaginative outputs.

Example Workflow:

1. **Data Collection:** Gather a diverse dataset of dream-like images and narratives.

2. **Model Training:** Train the GAN on this dataset, allowing the generator to learn and create dream visuals and narratives.

3. **Integration:** Implement the trained GAN into the dream interface system, where it dynamically generates dream content based on user inputs and mental states.

4. **Feedback Loop:** Continuously update and refine the GAN models based on user interactions and feedback to improve the dream experience over time.

Chapter 3: Enhancing Emotional Interaction

Theme: Implementing emotional AI to personalize the dream experience.

Ethan:

"How do we ensure that the dream environment is tailored to each individual's emotions?"

Dr. Ava:

"We'll integrate Emotion AI, which uses natural language processing (NLP) and sentiment analysis to understand and react to user emotions. By analyzing voice tone, facial expressions, and text input, the AI can adjust the dream environment to match the user's emotional state."

Ethan:

"What kind of NLP techniques are involved?"

Dr. Ava:

"We'll use techniques like named entity recognition (NER) to identify key elements in the user's input and sentiment analysis to gauge emotional tone. Combining these methods will allow the AI to create more meaningful and personalized interactions."

Understanding Emotion AI and NLP

Emotion AI is a branch of artificial intelligence focused on interpreting and responding to human emotions. It enhances user experiences by adapting systems based on emotional input. Here's how Emotion AI works, particularly through the use of Natural Language Processing (NLP) and sentiment analysis:

1. Natural Language Processing (NLP)

NLP is a field of AI that enables machines to understand and interact with human language. It involves several key techniques:

1. **Named Entity Recognition (NER):**
   - **Purpose:** Identifies and categorizes key elements (entities) in text, such as names, locations, dates, and other relevant details.
   - **Application:** Helps the AI understand the context and specifics of what the user is discussing or feeling. For example, recognizing a user's mention of "vacation" and "beach" can inform the AI that the user might be in a relaxed or nostalgic mood.

2. **Part-of-Speech Tagging (POS):**
   - **Purpose:** Determines the grammatical role of each word in a sentence (e.g., noun, verb, adjective).
   - **Application:** Assists in understanding sentence structure and context, which is crucial for accurate interpretation of user input.

3. **Dependency Parsing:**
   - **Purpose:** Analyzes the grammatical structure of a sentence to understand the relationships between words.
   - **Application:** Enhances the AI's ability to grasp complex sentences and nuanced meanings.

4. **Named Entity Linking:**
   - **Purpose:** Connects identified entities to a knowledge base for more context.
   - **Application:** Helps the AI to provide more informed and relevant responses based on the entities mentioned.

2. Sentiment Analysis

Sentiment analysis is used to determine the emotional tone of a piece of text. It involves:

1. **Emotion Detection:**
   - **Purpose:** Identifies specific emotions such as happiness, sadness, anger, or fear.
   - **Application:** Allows the AI to tailor the dream environment to the user's current emotional state. For example, if the sentiment analysis detects sadness, the AI might create a comforting and soothing dream scenario.

2. **Polarity Analysis:**
   - **Purpose:** Measures the positive or negative orientation of the text.
   - **Application:** Helps the AI understand the general sentiment and adjust the dream experience accordingly.

3. **Aspect-Based Sentiment Analysis:**
   - **Purpose:** Analyzes sentiments related to specific aspects or features.
   - **Application:** Useful for fine-tuning the dream environment based on particular aspects of the user's experience, such as their preferences for certain dream elements.

3. Integration into the Dream Interface

1. **Voice Tone Analysis:**
   - **Purpose:** Detects emotional nuances in the user's voice.
   - **Application:** Helps the AI adjust the dream environment based on vocal cues, such as altering the dream setting if the user's tone suggests stress or excitement.

2. **Facial Expression Analysis:**
   - **Purpose:** Interprets emotions based on facial expressions using computer vision techniques.
   - **Application:** Provides real-time feedback on the user's emotional state, allowing dynamic adjustments to the dream environment.

3. **Text Input Analysis:**
   - **Purpose:** Analyzes text input for emotional content and context.
   - **Application:** Enhances the AI's ability to understand and react to user emotions through written communication.

4. **Real-Time Adjustment:**
   - **Purpose:** Continuously updates the dream environment based on ongoing emotional input.
   - **Application:** Ensures that the dream experience remains aligned with the user's evolving emotional state, providing a responsive and immersive experience.

Technical Insight:

Emotion AI leverages advanced NLP techniques to interpret and respond to human emotions. By integrating named entity recognition, sentiment analysis, and real-time feedback mechanisms, the AI can create a personalized and emotionally resonant dream experience. This approach enhances the interaction between the user and the dream environment, ensuring that the generated content aligns with the user's emotional needs and preferences.

Example Workflow:

1. **Data Collection:** Gather voice samples, facial expressions, and text inputs from users.

2. **Model Training:** Train NLP and sentiment analysis models on this data to accurately interpret emotional cues.
3. **Integration:** Implement these models into the dream interface system, enabling real-time emotional analysis and adjustment of the dream environment.
4. **Continuous Refinement:** Use user feedback to further refine the Emotion AI models, improving their accuracy and responsiveness over time.

Ethan:

"How do we ensure the accuracy and relevance of the emotional adjustments made by the AI?"

Dr. Ava:

"We'll continuously test and validate the system with diverse user groups to fine-tune the AI's responses. Regular updates and improvements based on real-world feedback will help maintain accuracy and relevance."

Ethan:

"Are there any ethical concerns we should be aware of?"

Dr. Ava:

"Absolutely. We need to ensure user privacy and consent. We should also be cautious about the potential for emotional manipulation and ensure that the system is used responsibly and ethically."

Technical Insight:

Ensuring the ethical use of Emotion AI involves implementing robust privacy protections, obtaining informed consent from users, and establishing guidelines for responsible use. Regular audits and adherence to ethical standards are essential for maintaining trust and integrity in the system.

This chapter delves into the implementation of Emotion AI to enhance the personalization of the dream experience. By utilizing advanced NLP techniques and real-time emotional analysis, the AI can create a responsive and tailored dream environment, reflecting the user's emotional state and preferences.

Chapter 4: Creating the Dream-to-Reality Bridge

Theme: Establishing a system that bridges the dream world with the physical world.

Ethan:

"How can we bridge the dream world with reality effectively?"

Dr. Ava:

"We'll develop an API that allows our dream environment to interact with real-world data. This system will use data integration techniques to synchronize dream experiences with real-world stimuli, creating a seamless experience."

Ethan:

"What technologies are involved in this integration?"

Dr. Ava:

"We'll use web APIs to fetch real-time data and IoT devices to gather environmental information. This data will be fed into our system, allowing the dream environment to adjust based on real-world inputs."

Understanding the Dream-to-Reality Bridge

To create a seamless interaction between the dream world and reality, several key technologies and techniques are involved. This chapter explores these technologies and how they work together to build the bridge between these two realms.

1. Web APIs (Application Programming Interfaces)

Definition:

APIs are sets of rules and protocols that allow different software systems to communicate and interact with each other. They enable the integration of external data and services into applications.

How They Work:

1. **Request-Response Model:**
    - **Request:** An API request is sent to a server, asking for specific data or services.
    - **Response:** The server processes the request and returns the relevant data or performs the requested action.

2. **Endpoints:**
    - **Purpose:** APIs have endpoints that define specific paths for accessing different functionalities or data.
    - **Application:** For integrating real-world data into the dream environment, we would use endpoints to fetch weather updates, news feeds, or social media information.

3. **Authentication:**
    - **Purpose:** Ensures secure access to the API.

- **Application:** Tokens or keys are used to authenticate requests, ensuring that only authorized systems can access the data.

Example:

To fetch real-time weather data, we might use an API from a weather service. The dream environment could then adjust its settings based on current weather conditions, such as changing the dream landscape to reflect sunny or rainy weather.

Technical Insight:

APIs facilitate communication between different systems by defining specific methods and endpoints for data exchange. Authentication ensures that only authorized requests are processed, protecting data and system integrity.

---

2. IoT (Internet of Things) Devices

Definition:

IoT devices are physical objects embedded with sensors, software, and connectivity that allow them to collect and exchange data.

How They Work:

1. **Sensors:**
   - **Purpose:** Collect data from the physical environment, such as temperature, humidity, or light levels.
   - **Application:** Data from these sensors can be used to adjust the dream environment in real-time.

2. **Connectivity:**
   - **Purpose:** Enables IoT devices to communicate with other systems and networks.
   - **Application:** IoT devices send collected data to the central system, which integrates this data with the dream environment.

3. **Data Integration:**
   - **Purpose:** Combines data from multiple sources to create a unified view.

- **Application:** Data from IoT devices and APIs is integrated to adjust the dream environment based on real-world conditions.

Example:

A smart thermostat could provide temperature data to the system. If the thermostat detects a drop in temperature, the dream environment might simulate a cozy, warm setting to match the real-world conditions.

Technical Insight:

IoT devices use sensors to gather environmental data and connectivity to transmit this information to a central system. Data integration from IoT devices allows for dynamic adjustments in the dream environment based on real-world conditions.

---

3. Data Integration Techniques

Definition:

Data integration involves combining data from different sources to provide a unified view or to enable interoperability between systems.

How It Works:

1. **Data Aggregation:**
   - **Purpose:** Collects and combines data from multiple sources.
   - **Application:** Aggregates data from APIs and IoT devices to create a comprehensive picture of the user's environment.

2. **Data Mapping:**
   - **Purpose:** Ensures that data from different sources is compatible and correctly aligned.
   - **Application:** Maps real-world data to corresponding elements in the dream environment, such as associating weather conditions with dream settings.

3. **Real-Time Synchronization:**
   - **Purpose:** Updates data continuously to reflect current conditions.
   - **Application:** Adjusts the dream environment in real-time based on live data from APIs and IoT devices.

Example:

By integrating data from a variety of sources (e.g., weather APIs, smart home devices), the dream environment can be dynamically adjusted to reflect current real-world conditions, providing a seamless and immersive experience.

Technical Insight:

Data integration techniques involve aggregating and mapping data from multiple sources to create a cohesive view. Real-time synchronization ensures that the dream environment remains aligned with current real-world conditions, enhancing user experience.

Example Workflow:

1. **Data Collection:**
   - Use IoT devices to gather environmental data and APIs to fetch real-time information.

2. **Data Integration:**
   - Aggregate and map data from different sources to create a unified view.

3. **Real-Time Adjustment:**
   - Continuously update the dream environment based on live data, ensuring alignment with real-world conditions.

4. **User Interaction:**
   - Allow users to interact with the dream environment and provide feedback, refining the system over time.

Ethan:

"So, how do we ensure that the integration remains seamless and doesn't disrupt the user experience?"

Dr. Ava:

"We'll implement robust error handling and synchronization mechanisms to ensure smooth integration. Additionally, continuous testing and user feedback will help us identify and address any issues."

Ethan:

"Are there any challenges we should anticipate in this integration process?"

Dr. Ava:

"Certainly. One challenge is ensuring real-time data accuracy and consistency. We'll need to account for potential latency and data discrepancies. Additionally, maintaining user privacy and data security is crucial."

Technical Insight:

Challenges in integrating dream and reality include managing real-time data accuracy, addressing latency, and ensuring data privacy. By implementing strong error handling, synchronization mechanisms, and security measures, these challenges can be effectively addressed.

Summary:

This chapter explores the creation of a system that bridges the dream world with reality using APIs and IoT devices. By integrating real-world data with the dream environment, the system offers a seamless and adaptive experience, enhancing the overall dream experience with real-time inputs. The combination of web APIs, IoT devices, and data integration techniques creates a responsive and immersive dream environment, reflecting current real-world conditions and ensuring a harmonious interaction between the two realms.

Chapter 5: Learning from Feedback

Theme: Implementing feedback mechanisms to refine the AI's performance.

Ethan:

"How do we ensure that the AI continues to improve its understanding and performance?"

Dr. Ava:

"We'll use a feedback loop system where users provide ratings and comments on their dream experiences. This feedback will be used to retrain the AI, refining its algorithms and improving the quality of the dream interactions."

Ethan:

"How does this retraining process work?"

Dr. Ava:

"We'll employ supervised learning, where the AI is trained on labeled data, using the feedback as new training examples. The AI's performance is evaluated and adjusted based on this input, enhancing its ability to create better dream experiences."

Understanding Feedback Mechanisms and Supervised Learning

To ensure that the AI in the dream environment continues to evolve and improve, implementing a feedback loop is crucial. This chapter delves into how feedback mechanisms work and how supervised learning can be used to refine AI performance.

1. Feedback Loop System

Definition:

A feedback loop system involves collecting user feedback to improve a process or system. In the context of AI, it means using input from users to continuously enhance the AI's performance.

How It Works:

1. **User Feedback Collection:**
    - **Method:** Users rate their dream experiences and provide comments on various aspects, such as content relevance, emotional impact, and overall satisfaction.
    - **Application:** This feedback is gathered through surveys, in-app forms, or direct interactions within the dream environment.

2. **Feedback Analysis:**
    - **Method:** Analyzing the feedback to identify patterns, common issues, and areas for improvement.
    - **Application:** This involves processing the feedback to understand user preferences, detect errors, and pinpoint areas where the AI may be lacking.

3. **Incorporation into Training Data:**
    - **Method:** Incorporating feedback into the training dataset as new examples for the AI.
    - **Application:** Feedback is used to label data or adjust existing labels, helping the AI learn from real user experiences and preferences.

Example:

If users frequently report that the dream environment is too dark or unsettling, this feedback will be used to adjust the AI's algorithms to create more balanced and pleasing dream settings.

2. Supervised Learning

Definition:

Supervised learning is a machine learning approach where an AI model is trained on a dataset with known labels. The model learns to make predictions or decisions based on this labeled data.

How It Works:

1. **Training with Labeled Data:**
   - **Method:** The AI is trained on a dataset where each input has a corresponding correct output (label). For instance, user feedback on dream experiences can serve as labels for training.
   - **Application:** The AI learns to associate certain features of the dream environment with positive or negative feedback.

2. **Feedback as New Training Examples:**
   - **Method:** User feedback is used to generate new training examples or update existing ones.
   - **Application:** Feedback on specific dream elements, like the atmosphere or storyline, helps refine the AI's understanding and response mechanisms.

3. **Performance Evaluation and Adjustment:**
   - **Method:** Regularly evaluating the AI's performance based on its ability to correctly predict or generate desired outcomes.
   - **Application:** Adjusting the AI's algorithms and parameters based on performance metrics to improve accuracy and relevance.

Example:

If users rate dream settings based on their emotional responses, this data helps the AI learn which types of settings evoke positive emotions and which do not. The AI then adjusts its algorithms to enhance dream experiences accordingly.

Technical Insight:

1. **Feedback Loop Implementation:**

- **Collect Data:** Gather user feedback on dream experiences.
- **Analyze:** Process and analyze feedback to identify patterns and areas for improvement.
- **Integrate:** Use feedback to update the training data and refine the AI's models.

2. **Supervised Learning Process:**
   - **Data Preparation:** Label feedback data and integrate it into the training set.
   - **Training:** Use supervised learning algorithms to train the AI with labeled data.
   - **Evaluation:** Assess the AI's performance and make necessary adjustments based on feedback.

Ethan:

"So, how do we ensure that the integration remains seamless and doesn't disrupt the user experience?"

Dr. Ava:

"We'll implement robust error handling and synchronization mechanisms to ensure smooth integration. Additionally, continuous testing and user feedback will help us identify and address any issues."

Ethan:

"Are there any challenges we should anticipate in this integration process?"

Dr. Ava:

"Certainly. One challenge is ensuring real-time data accuracy and consistency. We'll need to account for potential latency and data discrepancies. Additionally, maintaining user privacy and data security is crucial."

Summary:

This chapter explores the role of feedback mechanisms in refining AI performance through supervised learning. By implementing a feedback loop system, user input is used to continuously improve the AI's ability to create more accurate and engaging dream experiences. Supervised learning ensures that the AI model is trained effectively using labeled feedback data, enhancing its predictive capabilities and overall performance.

Chapter 6: The Ethics of Dream AI

Theme: Exploring the ethical implications of integrating AI into personal dreamscapes.

Ethan:

"What are the ethical considerations of using AI to influence dreams?"

Dr. Ava:

"We must address privacy concerns, data security, and the potential for misuse. Ensuring user consent and safeguarding personal data are crucial. Additionally, we need to consider the psychological impacts of AI-driven dream manipulation."

Ethan:

"How can we mitigate these risks?"

Dr. Ava:

"Implementing robust data protection measures, transparent consent protocols, and regular ethical reviews will help mitigate these risks. Engaging with ethicists and mental health professionals will also ensure that our system is used responsibly."

Understanding the Ethics of Dream AI

The integration of AI into personal dreamscapes raises significant ethical questions. This chapter explores the ethical considerations associated with dream AI and how to address them responsibly.

1. Privacy and Data Security

Privacy Concerns:

- **Definition:** Privacy involves protecting personal information from unauthorized access or misuse.
- **Considerations:** With AI influencing dreams, sensitive personal data, such as emotional responses and dream content, could be collected. This raises concerns about how this data is stored, accessed, and used.

Data Security:

- **Definition:** Data security involves safeguarding data from breaches and unauthorized access.
- **Measures:**
  - **Encryption:** Encrypting data both in transit and at rest to prevent unauthorized access.
  - **Access Control:** Implementing strict access controls to ensure only authorized personnel can view or manipulate sensitive data.
  - **Regular Audits:** Conducting regular security audits to identify and address vulnerabilities.

Example:

Implementing end-to-end encryption ensures that dream data transmitted between the user's device and the AI server remains confidential and secure from potential breaches.

---

2. Informed Consent

Definition:

Informed consent involves ensuring that users are fully aware of and agree to the data collection and AI manipulation of their dream experiences.

Consent Protocols:

- **Transparency:** Clearly communicate what data is collected, how it will be used, and any potential risks.
- **User Control:** Allow users to opt in or out of specific features and revoke consent at any time.
- **Clear Documentation:** Provide easy-to-understand documentation about the AI system's operations and data handling practices.

Example:

Before using the AI system, users should receive a comprehensive overview of how their dream data will be used and have the option to adjust their privacy settings or discontinue participation.

3. Psychological Impact

Definition:

The psychological impact involves the effects that AI-driven dream manipulation can have on a user's mental health and well-being.

Considerations:

- **Emotional Well-being:** Ensure that AI interventions do not negatively affect users' emotional health or cause distress.
- **Professional Oversight:** Collaborate with mental health professionals to assess and manage potential psychological impacts.
- **Ethical Reviews:** Conduct regular ethical reviews to evaluate the impact of the AI system on users' mental health.

Example:

Incorporating feedback from mental health professionals helps to ensure that dream manipulation is supportive and therapeutic rather than harmful or intrusive.

4. Preventing Misuse

Definition:

Preventing misuse involves safeguarding the AI system from being used for unethical purposes or by unauthorized individuals.

Measures:

- **Access Control:** Implement stringent access controls to prevent unauthorized use of the AI system.
- **Ethical Guidelines:** Develop and enforce guidelines for ethical use, ensuring that the AI system is used in accordance with agreed-upon standards.
- **Monitoring and Reporting:** Establish mechanisms for monitoring the use of the AI system and reporting any misuse or ethical concerns.

Example:

Creating a secure authentication process for accessing the AI system helps to prevent unauthorized individuals from manipulating user dreams or accessing sensitive data.

Technical Insight:

Ethical AI practices involve several key components:

1. **Data Protection:**
    - **Encryption** and **Access Control** ensure the security and confidentiality of user data.
    - **Regular Audits** help identify and address potential vulnerabilities.
2. **Informed Consent:**
    - **Transparency** and **User Control** are essential for obtaining and maintaining user consent.
    - **Clear Documentation** provides users with the necessary information to make informed decisions.
3. **Psychological Impact:**

- **Collaboration** with mental health professionals and **Ethical Reviews** ensure that AI-driven dream manipulation is supportive and not harmful.

4. **Preventing Misuse:**
   - **Access Control** and **Ethical Guidelines** prevent unauthorized use and ensure responsible operation of the AI system.

Example Workflow:

1. **Implement Data Protection:**
   - Encrypt and control access to dream data.
   - Conduct regular security audits.

2. **Ensure Informed Consent:**
   - Provide transparency and allow user control over data usage.
   - Maintain clear and comprehensive documentation.

3. **Monitor Psychological Impact:**
   - Collaborate with mental health professionals.
   - Conduct ethical reviews to assess the impact of dream manipulation.

4. **Prevent Misuse:**
   - Implement secure authentication and enforce ethical guidelines.
   - Monitor usage and report any concerns.

Ethan:

"So, how do we ensure that the integration remains seamless and doesn't disrupt the user experience?"

Dr. Ava:

"We'll implement robust error handling and synchronization mechanisms to ensure smooth integration. Additionally, continuous testing and user feedback will help us identify and address any issues."

Ethan:

"Are there any challenges we should anticipate in this integration process?"

Dr. Ava:

"Certainly. One challenge is ensuring real-time data accuracy and consistency. We'll need to account for potential latency and data discrepancies. Additionally, maintaining user privacy and data security is crucial."

Summary:

This chapter explores the ethical considerations of integrating AI into personal dreamscapes, focusing on privacy, informed consent, psychological impact, and misuse prevention. By implementing robust data protection measures, transparent consent protocols, and ethical reviews, we can ensure that the AI system is used responsibly and respects user well-being. Engaging with ethicists and mental health professionals further supports the ethical use of AI in dream manipulation.

Chapter 7: Personalizing the Experience

Chapter 7: Personalizing the Experience

Theme: *Tailoring the AI's responses to individual preferences and needs.*

Ethan:

"How can we make sure the dream experiences are truly personalized for each user?"

Dr. Ava:

"By using machine learning models that analyze user preferences, past interactions, and feedback, we can create highly personalized dream environments. We'll implement clustering algorithms to group users with similar preferences and recommend tailored experiences."

Ethan:

"What role do clustering algorithms play here?"

Dr. Ava:

"Clustering algorithms, like K-means, group similar data points together. By analyzing user data, these algorithms help identify patterns and preferences, *allowing us to create personalized dream environments that match individual tastes."*

Understanding Personalization Through Machine Learning

Personalizing the AI's response to individual user preferences involves using machine learning techniques to analyze and adapt to user data. This chapter explores how clustering algorithms, particularly K-means, are employed to achieve personalization in dream experiences.

1. Machine Learning Models for Personalization

Definition:

Machine learning models use algorithms to learn from and make predictions based on data. For personalization, these models analyze user behavior and preferences to tailor experiences.

Key Components:

- ***Data Collection:*** *Gather data on user interactions, preferences, and feedback.*
- ***Feature Extraction:*** *Identify relevant features or characteristics from the data that influence user preferences.*
- ***Model Training:*** *Use historical data to train the model to predict user preferences and behaviors.*

Example:

An AI system might collect data on the types of dream environments users prefer (e.g., tranquil landscapes vs. dynamic adventures) and use this information to personalize future dream experiences.

---

2. Clustering Algorithms

Definition:

Clustering algorithms group similar data points based on specific features, helping to identify patterns and relationships within the data.

K-means Clustering:

- ***Purpose:*** *To partition data into distinct clusters based on similarities.*

- ***How It Works:***
    - ***Initialization:*** *Randomly select K centroids (cluster centers).*
    - ***Assignment:*** *Assign each data point to the nearest centroid.*
    - ***Update:*** *Recalculate centroids based on the mean of the assigned data points.*
    - ***Iteration:*** *Repeat assignment and update steps until convergence (centroids no longer change).*

Application:

By clustering users based on their dream preferences and feedback, the AI can create distinct user profiles and tailor dream environments to match each profile's characteristics.

Example:

If K-means clustering reveals that users fall into groups with preferences for serene vs. adventurous dreams, the AI can generate dream environments tailored to these distinct groups, enhancing personalization.

---

3. Implementing Personalization

User Data Collection:

- **Sources:** Collect data from user interactions with the AI system, including feedback, preferences, and behavioral patterns.
- **Storage:** Store data securely to ensure privacy and compliance with data protection regulations.

Data Analysis and Clustering:

- **Feature Extraction:** Identify key features that influence user preferences, such as preferred dream settings or emotional responses.
- **Clustering:** Apply K-means clustering to group users with similar preferences and characteristics.

Personalized Dream Environment:

- **Customization:** Tailor dream experiences based on the user's cluster. For example, users in a "tranquil" cluster might receive dreams set in *peaceful landscapes, while those in an "adventurous" cluster might experience dynamic and exciting environments.*

- **Feedback Integration:** *Continuously refine and adjust the personalization model based on user feedback to enhance accuracy and satisfaction.*

Example Workflow:

1. **Collect Data:**
   - *Gather user preferences and feedback.*
   - *Store data securely.*

2. **Analyze Data:**
   - *Extract features and apply K-means clustering.*
   - *Identify user clusters based on preferences.*

3. **Personalize Experiences:**
   - *Create tailored dream environments for each user cluster.*
   - *Adjust based on ongoing feedback.*

Technical Insight:

Personalizing dream experiences involves several steps:

1. **Machine Learning Models:** *Use models to analyze user data and predict preferences.*

2. **Clustering Algorithms:** *Apply K-means to group users based on similar preferences.*

3. **Tailored Experiences:** *Customize dream environments based on cluster characteristics.*

Challenges:

- **Data Quality:** *Ensure accurate and representative data collection.*
- **Privacy:** *Protect user data and ensure compliance with privacy regulations.*
- **Adaptability:** *Continuously update models to reflect changing user preferences.*

Example:

An AI system that personalizes dream experiences using K-means clustering might find that users with similar emotional responses and dream preferences are grouped together. By analyzing these clusters, the AI can tailor dream environments to meet each user's unique tastes, enhancing the overall experience.

Ethan:

"How do we ensure the personalization remains effective over time?"

Dr. Ava:

"We'll implement a feedback loop that continuously updates user profiles based on new interactions and feedback. This ongoing adjustment will help the AI stay aligned with evolving user preferences."

Ethan:

"How can we validate the effectiveness of our personalization?"

Dr. Ava:

"By monitoring user satisfaction and engagement metrics, we can assess the effectiveness of our personalization. Regular A/B testing and user surveys will also help us refine the system."

Summary:

This chapter explores how clustering algorithms like K-means are used to personalize dream experiences by analyzing user data and preferences. By implementing machine learning models and continuously updating user profiles based on feedback, the AI can create highly tailored and satisfying dream environments. Addressing challenges such as data quality and privacy ensures that personalization remains effective and user-centric.

Chapter 8: The Future of Integrated Worlds

Theme: Envisioning future advancements and applications of AI in dream and reality integration.

Ethan:

"What does the future hold for integrating dreams and reality with AI?"

Dr. Ava:

"The future promises even more sophisticated integrations, such as real-time dream monitoring, adaptive learning algorithms, and more immersive virtual environments. Advances in neurotechnology and AI will enable deeper connections between our dreams and reality."

Ethan:

"What advancements should we anticipate?"

Dr. Ava:

"Look forward to advancements in brain-computer interfaces, which will allow more direct interaction between the brain and AI systems. Enhanced natural language processing and emotional AI will also lead to more intuitive and responsive dream environments."

Exploring Future Advancements in AI-Driven Dream Integration

As we envision the future of integrating dreams with reality through AI, several cutting-edge technologies and advancements are on the horizon. This chapter explores these future trends, focusing on brain-computer interfaces, advanced NLP, and emotional AI.

1. Brain-Computer Interfaces (BCIs)

Definition:

Brain-computer interfaces (BCIs) are technologies that enable direct communication between the brain and external devices. BCIs can translate brain signals into commands or data, facilitating a more seamless interaction with AI systems.

How They Work:

- **Signal Acquisition:** Electrodes or other sensors capture brain activity, typically using EEG (electroencephalography) or implanted electrodes.
- **Signal Processing:** Raw brain signals are processed and decoded into meaningful data using signal processing algorithms.
- **Interaction:** The decoded data is used to control or interact with external devices, including AI systems.

Applications:

- **Real-Time Dream Monitoring:** BCIs could monitor brain activity during sleep, providing real-time data to enhance the dream environment dynamically.
- **Enhanced Interaction:** Directly influencing dream content or environment based on brain signals for a more immersive experience.

Example:

A BCI could detect when a user is experiencing a particular emotional state during sleep and adjust the dream environment accordingly, such as by enhancing relaxation or excitement based on the detected brain signals.

2. Advanced Natural Language Processing (NLP)

Definition:

Natural language processing (NLP) involves enabling machines to understand and interpret human language. Future advancements in NLP will improve the AI's ability to interact with users in a more natural and intuitive manner.

Key Advancements:

- **Contextual Understanding:** Improved algorithms for understanding context, nuances, and subtleties in language.
- **Conversational AI:** Enhanced dialogue systems that can engage in more complex and meaningful conversations, including understanding and responding to emotions.

Applications:

- **Intuitive Dream Interaction:** AI systems will be able to understand user inputs more effectively, creating more personalized and context-aware dream environments.
- **Natural Dialogue:** Engaging users in natural conversations about their dreams and preferences, leading to more tailored dream experiences.

Example:

An advanced NLP system could allow users to describe their dream preferences in natural language, and the AI would interpret these descriptions accurately to generate customized dream scenarios.

---

3. Enhanced Emotional AI

Definition:

Emotional AI involves creating systems that can recognize, interpret, and respond to human emotions. Future advancements will improve the AI's ability to detect and react to a wide range of emotional cues.

Key Advancements:

- **Multimodal Emotion Recognition:** Integration of data from various sources, such as voice, facial expressions, and physiological signals, to accurately assess emotional states.
- **Adaptive Responses:** AI systems that can adjust responses and interactions based on detected emotions, providing a more empathetic and engaging experience.

Applications:

- **Responsive Dream Environments:** AI will be able to adapt dream environments in real-time based on the user's emotional state, enhancing the overall experience.
- **Emotional Support:** Providing emotional support or therapy through dream environments tailored to address specific emotional needs.

Example:

An emotional AI system could detect when a user is feeling anxious or stressed and adjust the dream environment to include calming elements, such as serene landscapes or soothing sounds.

Technical Insight

Brain-Computer Interfaces (BCIs):

BCIs represent a significant advancement in direct brain-AI interaction. By capturing and interpreting brain signals, BCIs can provide real-time feedback and control, enhancing the integration of dreams and reality.

Natural Language Processing (NLP):

Future improvements in NLP will enable more sophisticated and natural interactions between users and AI. Enhanced understanding of context and emotions will make dream environments more responsive and personalized.

Emotional AI:

Advancements in emotional AI will allow for more nuanced and empathetic interactions. By integrating multimodal data, AI systems can better understand and respond to user emotions, creating more tailored and supportive dream experiences.

Ethan:

"What challenges might we face as we move towards these advancements?"

Dr. Ava:

"Challenges include ensuring the accuracy and reliability of BCI systems, handling the complexity of advanced NLP, and addressing ethical concerns related to emotional AI. We'll need to invest in research, testing, and ethical considerations to overcome these hurdles."

Ethan:

"How can we prepare for these future developments?"

Dr. Ava:

"Staying at the forefront of research, collaborating with experts in neurotechnology, AI, and ethics, and continuously testing and refining our systems will help us navigate these advancements. Being proactive in addressing potential challenges will also be crucial."

Summary:

Chapter 8 explores the future of integrating dreams and reality through AI, focusing on advancements such as brain-computer interfaces, improved natural language processing, and enhanced emotional AI. These technologies promise to deepen the connection between dreams and reality, creating more immersive and personalized experiences. Addressing challenges and preparing for future developments will be key to successfully implementing these advancements and achieving a harmonious integration of dreams and reality.

Chapter 9: Reflections on the Journey

Theme: Reflecting on the impact of integrating AI into dream worlds and its implications for the future.

Ethan:

"What have we learned from this journey?"

Dr. Ava:

"We've learned that integrating AI with dreams and reality can enhance our understanding of both realms, leading to richer experiences and new possibilities. Our work illustrates the potential of AI to transform personal and creative experiences, bridging the gap between imagination and reality."

Ethan:

"What are the key takeaways?"

Dr. Ava:

"The key takeaways include the importance of ethical considerations, the power of AI to personalize experiences, and the potential for future advancements to further integrate and enrich our lives. Our journey shows that AI can not only reflect but also enhance our deepest experiences."

Reflecting on the Journey

As we reflect on the journey of integrating AI into dream worlds, several key insights and implications emerge. This chapter delves into the transformative impact of this technology, emphasizing ethical considerations, personalization, and future advancements.

1. The Transformative Power of AI

Enhancing Understanding:

- **Personal and Creative Experiences:** AI has the capability to deepen our understanding of personal experiences and creative expression. By merging dreams with reality, AI provides new avenues for exploring and enhancing our inner world.

- **Bridging Imagination and Reality:** AI acts as a bridge between our imaginative and physical realms, allowing us to experience and interact with our dreams in unprecedented ways.

Example:

An artist using AI to translate dream imagery into digital art can gain new insights into their creative process, while individuals can explore personal dreams to uncover hidden emotions or inspirations.

---

2. Ethical Considerations

Privacy and Data Security:

- **Protecting Personal Information:** Integrating AI with dreams involves sensitive data, making privacy and security paramount. Ensuring robust data protection measures and obtaining informed consent are crucial.

- **Responsible Use:** Ethical considerations extend to how AI influences personal experiences. It's important to prevent misuse and ensure that AI systems are used responsibly and with respect for user autonomy.

Example:

Implementing encryption and secure access protocols ensures that users' dream data is protected. Transparent consent mechanisms and regular audits help maintain ethical standards.

3. Personalization of Experiences

Tailoring Interactions:

- **Adaptive Dream Environments:** AI's ability to analyze user preferences and feedback allows for highly personalized dream experiences. By adapting environments to individual needs, AI enhances the relevance and impact of dreams.
- **Clustering and Recommendations:** Advanced machine learning techniques enable AI to group users with similar preferences and offer tailored experiences, enriching the overall experience.

Example:

A user who frequently dreams about nature can have their dream environment adjusted to include serene landscapes, tailored to their specific preferences and emotional states.

4. Future Advancements

Next-Generation Technologies:

- **Brain-Computer Interfaces (BCIs):** Future developments in BCIs will enable even more direct and immersive interactions between the brain and AI systems, further blurring the lines between dreams and reality.
- **Enhanced NLP and Emotional AI:** Improvements in natural language processing and emotional AI will make interactions more intuitive and responsive, creating richer and more personalized dream environments.

Example:

BCI technology could allow users to influence their dream settings through thought alone, while advanced NLP systems could engage in complex, empathetic conversations with users about their dreams and preferences.

Technical Insight

The integration of AI into personal experiences reveals the potential for AI to transform creativity and understanding. By bridging the gap between imagination and reality, AI enhances personal and creative experiences, highlighting the importance of ethical considerations, personalization, and future advancements.

Key Takeaways:

1. **Ethical Considerations:** Safeguarding privacy and ensuring responsible use are crucial for maintaining trust and ensuring positive outcomes.

2. **Personalization:** AI's ability to tailor experiences to individual preferences enhances the relevance and impact of interactions, enriching the user experience.

3. **Future Advancements:** Emerging technologies such as BCIs and advanced NLP promise to further enhance the integration of dreams and reality, offering new possibilities for exploration and connection.

Ethan:

"What are the next steps for us as we move forward?"

Dr. Ava:

"Our next steps involve continuing to refine our systems, addressing ethical challenges proactively, and exploring new technologies to further enhance the integration of dreams and reality. Ongoing research and collaboration with experts will help us navigate these advancements and ensure that we use AI responsibly."

Ethan:

"How can we ensure that our work remains impactful and beneficial?"

Dr. Ava:

"By staying committed to ethical principles, focusing on user needs and experiences, and embracing innovation while addressing potential challenges, we can ensure that our work remains impactful and beneficial. Continuous feedback and adaptation will be key to our success."

Summary:

Chapter 9 reflects on the journey of integrating AI into dream worlds, emphasizing the transformative potential of this technology. Key insights include the importance of ethical considerations, the power of AI to personalize experiences, and the promise of future advancements. The chapter underscores the impact of AI on bridging imagination and reality, highlighting the need for ongoing research, ethical vigilance, and user-centered design.

Chapter 10: Beyond the Interface

Theme: Embracing the future possibilities of AI and dream integration.

Ethan:

"How do we continue to push the boundaries of what AI can achieve with dream integration?"

Dr. Ava:

"We continue to innovate and explore new technologies. By staying at the forefront of AI research and maintaining a focus on user experience and ethical practices, we can unlock new possibilities and create even more immersive and meaningful dream environments."

Ethan:

"What is the ultimate vision for this technology?"

Dr. Ava:

"The ultimate vision is a world where AI seamlessly blends with our imagination and reality, enhancing our experiences and expanding our horizons. It's about creating a harmonious coexistence where both realms enrich each other, leading to a more fulfilling and inspired life."

Embracing Future Possibilities

As we look to the future of AI and dream integration, several exciting possibilities and directions emerge. This chapter explores how we can continue to innovate and expand the boundaries of this technology, focusing on new advancements and their potential impacts.

1. Advancements in Neurotechnology

Brain-Computer Interfaces (BCIs):

- **Direct Brain Interaction:** BCIs offer a direct line of communication between the brain and AI systems, enabling users to influence their dream environments through thoughts and neural signals.

- **Enhanced Immersion:** Future BCIs could allow for a more immersive experience by translating complex brain activity into dynamic dream environments, offering unprecedented levels of control and personalization.

Example:

A BCI could enable users to modify their dream settings in real-time by simply thinking about desired changes, such as altering the dreamscape or interacting with dream characters.

2. Evolving Natural Language Processing (NLP)

Contextual Understanding:

- **Deep Conversational AI:** Advanced NLP will enable AI to engage in more nuanced and context-aware conversations with users, understanding and responding to complex emotional and thematic elements in dreams.

- **Adaptive Storytelling:** Improved NLP can facilitate dynamic storytelling within dreams, creating narratives that adapt to user preferences and evolving emotional states.

Example:

An AI system could craft a personalized dream narrative that evolves based on ongoing user interactions and feedback, creating a more engaging and relevant dream experience.

3. Enhanced Emotional AI

Emotion Recognition and Response:

- **Subtle Emotional Cues:** Future developments in emotional AI will allow for even finer detection of emotional cues, enabling the system to create more accurate and responsive dream environments.
- **Emotional Resilience:** By understanding and addressing emotional challenges, AI could help users navigate and resolve emotional issues within their dreams, promoting psychological well-being.

Example:

An AI could detect signs of stress or anxiety in a user's dream and adjust the environment to provide calming or therapeutic experiences, tailored to the user's needs.

4. Expanding Creative Possibilities

Generative Art and Music:

- **Dream-Based Art Creation:** AI could generate artwork or music inspired by users' dreams, translating dream experiences into creative expressions that enhance personal and artistic fulfillment.
- **Collaborative Creativity:** Users and AI could collaborate in real-time to create unique dreamscapes, blending human creativity with AI's generative capabilities.

Example:

A user's dream about a fantastical landscape could inspire an AI to generate a piece of digital art or music that reflects the visual and emotional elements of the dream.

Technical Insight

The future of AI and dream integration involves embracing advancements in neurotechnology, NLP, emotional AI, and creative tools. These innovations promise to create more immersive, personalized, and meaningful dream experiences by bridging imagination and reality. Key areas of focus include:

- **BCIs for Direct Brain Interaction:** Enhancing user control and immersion.
- **Advanced NLP for Contextual Conversations:** Facilitating dynamic storytelling and user engagement.
- **Refined Emotional AI for Better Emotional Support:** Addressing and adapting to subtle emotional cues.
- **Generative Art and Music for Expanded Creative Possibilities:** Translating dreams into creative outputs.

Ethan:

"How can we ensure that these advancements remain beneficial and align with our core values?"

Dr. Ava:

"By continuing to prioritize ethical considerations, user-centric design, and transparency in our development processes, we can ensure that these advancements are used responsibly and effectively. Engaging with diverse stakeholders and maintaining an open dialogue about the impacts of our technology will be crucial."

Ethan:

"What role will ongoing research and collaboration play in shaping this future?"

Dr. Ava:

"Ongoing research and collaboration will be vital in driving innovation and addressing emerging challenges. By working with experts in AI, neuroscience, ethics, and user experience, we can develop solutions that enhance the integration of dreams and reality while safeguarding user well-being."

Summary:

Chapter 10 envisions the future of AI and dream integration, highlighting the exciting possibilities and advancements on the horizon. From brain-computer interfaces to enhanced natural language processing and emotional AI, the chapter explores how these innovations can create more immersive and personalized dream experiences. By focusing on ethical practices and ongoing research, we can ensure that these technologies enrich our lives while maintaining a harmonious balance between imagination and reality.

Conclusion

The novel *"Beyond the Interface"* offers a captivating narrative interwoven with technical insights into the integration of AI and dream worlds. As readers journey through Ethan's and Dr. Ava's groundbreaking project, they are not only drawn into a story of innovation and discovery but are also introduced to the complex technologies that make such advancements possible.

Through engaging dialogues and detailed technical explanations, the novel demystifies the intricate workings of AI and machine learning. Readers gain an understanding of key concepts such as neural networks, GANs, emotion AI, APIs, and data integration techniques. Each chapter blends the personal and technical aspects, making the learning process seamless and enjoyable.

Key Takeaways:

1. **Understanding AI and Machine Learning:** The novel provides a clear explanation of fundamental AI technologies, including neural networks, reinforcement learning, and clustering algorithms. Readers learn how these technologies are applied to create immersive dream environments and personalize experiences.

2. **Ethical Considerations:** The ethical implications of AI in personal dreamscapes are explored in depth. Topics such as data privacy, user consent, and potential psychological impacts are addressed, highlighting the importance of responsible AI development.

3. **Future Possibilities:** The book looks ahead to future advancements in AI and dream integration, such as brain-computer interfaces and enhanced emotional AI. It encourages readers to envision how these technologies could shape our interactions with both dreams and reality.

4. **Practical Applications:** By illustrating how AI can be applied to real-world scenarios, the novel helps readers understand the potential of these technologies to transform creativity, personal experiences, and emotional well-being.

In Summary:

"Beyond the Interface" is more than just a narrative; it is an educational journey through the realms of AI and its applications in blending dreams with reality. Through its rich storytelling and technical insights, the novel offers a unique learning experience that both informs and inspires. Readers are left with a deeper appreciation of how AI technologies work and their potential to create new, enriching experiences at the intersection of imagination and reality.

A glossary of 50 key terms related to AI, machine learning, and the novel's concepts:

1. **AI (Artificial Intelligence)**: The simulation of human intelligence processes by machines, particularly computer systems.

2. **Machine Learning**: A subset of AI where algorithms learn from and make predictions based on data.

3. **Neural Networks**: Computational models inspired by the human brain, consisting of interconnected nodes (neurons) that process data.

4. **Deep Learning**: A subset of machine learning that uses neural networks with many layers to analyze complex patterns in data.

5. **Reinforcement Learning**: A type of machine learning where an agent learns to make decisions by receiving rewards or penalties for its actions.

6. **GANs (Generative Adversarial Networks)**: A type of neural network where two networks (generator and discriminator) work against each other to create realistic data.

7. **NLP (Natural Language Processing)**: A field of AI that enables machines to understand, interpret, and generate human language.

8. **Sentiment Analysis**: The use of NLP to determine the sentiment or emotion expressed in text.

9. **Emotion AI**: AI that detects and responds to human emotions using various inputs, such as text, voice, or facial expressions.

10. **Clustering Algorithms**: Algorithms that group similar data points together, such as K-means clustering.

11. **K-means**: A clustering algorithm that partitions data into K distinct clusters based on feature similarity.

12. **APIs (Application Programming Interfaces)**: Sets of rules that allow different software systems to communicate and interact.

13. **IoT (Internet of Things)**: A network of physical objects embedded with sensors and connectivity that collect and exchange data.

14. **Web API**: An API that provides access to web-based services and data.

15. **Real-Time Data**: Information that is collected and processed instantly, reflecting current conditions.

16. **Data Integration**: The process of combining data from multiple sources to create a unified view.

17. **Supervised Learning**: A machine learning approach where the model is trained on labeled data to make predictions or classify data.

18. **Unsupervised Learning**: A machine learning approach where the model learns patterns from unlabeled data.

19. **Data Aggregation**: Collecting and combining data from various sources to provide comprehensive insights.

20. **Data Mapping**: Aligning data from different sources to ensure compatibility and accurate representation.

21. **Real-Time Synchronization**: Continuously updating data to reflect current conditions and ensure consistency.

22. **Brain-Computer Interfaces (BCIs)**: Technology that enables direct communication between the brain and external devices.

23. **Feedback Loop**: A system where outputs are fed back into the system as inputs to improve performance.

24. **Ethical AI**: Principles and practices that ensure AI systems are used responsibly and ethically.

25. **User Consent**: The process of obtaining permission from users before collecting or using their data.

26. **Data Security**: Measures and protocols to protect data from unauthorized access or breaches.

27. **Privacy Concerns**: Issues related to the protection of personal information and ensuring user privacy.

28. **Transparency**: The practice of making AI processes and decisions understandable and open to scrutiny.

29. **Neurotechnology**: Technology that interacts with the nervous system to enhance or repair brain functions.

30. **Sentiment**: The emotional tone or attitude expressed in text or speech.

31. **Named Entity Recognition (NER)**: A technique in NLP that identifies and classifies entities such as names, dates, and locations in text.

32. **Adaptive Learning Algorithms**: Algorithms that adjust their learning processes based on new data or changing conditions.

33. **Virtual Environment**: A computer-generated space where users can interact with digital objects and scenarios.

34. **Generative Models**: AI models that create new data based on learned patterns from existing data.

35. **Imaginative Content**: Creative and novel material generated by AI, often used in dream environments.

36. **User Experience (UX)**: The overall experience and satisfaction of users interacting with a system or product.

37. **Robust Error Handling**: Techniques for managing and mitigating errors in software systems to ensure stability and reliability.

38. **Ethical Reviews**: Evaluations of AI systems to ensure they adhere to ethical standards and practices.

39. **User Interaction**: The ways in which users engage with and influence a system or application.

40. **Machine Learning Model**: A mathematical framework or algorithm used to make predictions or decisions based on data.

41. **Data Privacy**: The protection of personal data from unauthorized access or use.

42. **Harmonious Coexistence**: The integration of different systems or elements in a way that creates a balanced and effective outcome.

43. **Innovative Technologies**: New and advanced technologies that push the boundaries of current capabilities.

44. **Immersive Experience**: A highly engaging and interactive experience that fully captivates users.

45. **Creative Enhancement**: The use of technology to augment or inspire creative processes and outputs.

46. **System Synchronization**: The process of aligning different components or systems to work together seamlessly.

47. **Personalization**: Customizing experiences or interactions based on individual preferences and characteristics.

48. **Predictive Algorithms**: Algorithms that forecast future outcomes based on historical data and trends.

49. **Emotional Response**: Reactions and feelings elicited by interactions with a system or environment.

50. **Data Retraining**: Updating and improving machine learning models based on new data and feedback.

Eternal Reverie and **Beyond the Interface** collectively weave a narrative that explores the integration of dreams and reality through advanced technology. These two novels, though distinct in their focus, offer a comprehensive view of the potential and challenges associated with merging these two realms. Here's a detailed summary that encapsulates the essence of both:

Eternal Reverie introduces Ethan, a visionary writer, who embarks on an ambitious quest to blend his dream world with reality. As Ethan explores the possibility of creating a seamless interface between dreams and everyday life, he is joined by his partner, Lila, and an AI named Ava. The story unfolds in ten chapters, each addressing different facets of this integration journey.

Chapter 1: The Vision of Dual Worlds

Ethan's dream is to create a world where his imaginative dreamscapes can interact with reality. Dr. Ava, an AI expert, explains that achieving this requires a sophisticated AI capable of understanding and enhancing human dreams. The technical approach involves using neural networks for learning dream patterns and reinforcement learning for optimizing AI responses based on user feedback.

Chapter 2: Building the Dream Interface

The technical foundation is laid with Generative Adversarial Networks (GANs), which consist of a generator and a discriminator working in tandem to create and refine dream-like visuals and narratives. This technology allows for the generation of realistic or imaginative content by iteratively improving the outputs based on feedback from the discriminator.

Chapter 3: Enhancing Emotional Interaction

To tailor the dream environment to individual emotions, Emotion AI is employed. This involves natural language processing (NLP) and sentiment analysis to understand and react to user emotions. Techniques like named entity recognition (NER) and sentiment analysis enable the AI to adjust the dream environment based on voice tone, facial expressions, and text input.

Chapter 4: Creating the Dream-to-Reality Bridge

A crucial development is the creation of an API to synchronize the dream environment with real-world data. Using web APIs and IoT devices, real-time data such as weather conditions or room temperature can influence the dreamscape. Data integration techniques ensure that real-world stimuli are accurately reflected in the dream environment.

Chapter 5: Learning from Feedback

The AI's performance is refined through a feedback loop system where users provide ratings and comments on their dream experiences. This feedback is used in a supervised learning process to retrain the AI, enhancing its ability to create more personalized and satisfying dream experiences.

Chapter 6: The Ethics of Dream AI

Ethical considerations are paramount in integrating AI with dreams. Privacy concerns, data security, and the potential for misuse are addressed through robust data protection measures, transparent consent protocols, and regular ethical reviews. Engaging with ethicists and mental health professionals helps ensure responsible use of the technology.

Chapter 7: Personalizing the Experience

Machine learning models are used to personalize the dream experience based on user preferences, past interactions, and feedback. Clustering algorithms, such as K-means, help identify patterns and preferences among users, allowing for tailored dream environments that cater to individual tastes.

Chapter 8: The Future of Integrated Worlds

The future holds promise for even more sophisticated integrations, including real-time dream monitoring and advanced neurotechnology. Brain-computer interfaces, enhanced NLP, and emotional AI are anticipated to deepen the connection between dreams and reality, creating more immersive and responsive dream environments.

Chapter 9: Reflections on the Journey

Reflecting on the journey, Ethan and Dr. Ava recognize the profound impact of integrating AI with dreams and reality. The work demonstrates AI's potential to enhance personal and creative experiences, bridging the gap between imagination and reality while highlighting the importance of ethical considerations and personalization.

Chapter 10: Beyond the Interface

The ultimate vision is a world where AI seamlessly blends with imagination and reality. Continuous innovation and a focus on user experience and ethical practices will drive future advancements, creating a harmonious coexistence where dreams and reality enrich each other.

Beyond the Interface complements **Eternal Reverie** by providing a detailed exploration of the technical and ethical aspects of AI integration with dreams. It delves into how AI technologies, including neural networks, GANs, and Emotion AI, are used to create and refine dream environments. Through technical dialogues, the novel educates readers about the inner workings of these technologies and their applications in enhancing personal experiences.

Chapter Summaries:

Chapter 1: The Vision of Dual Worlds – Introduces the concept of integrating dreams and reality through AI, focusing on neural networks and reinforcement learning.

Chapter 2: Building the Dream Interface – Explores Generative Adversarial Networks (GANs) for creating realistic dreamscapes.

Chapter 3: Enhancing Emotional Interaction – Details the use of Emotion AI, NLP, and sentiment analysis to personalize dream experiences.

Chapter 4: Creating the Dream-to-Reality Bridge – Discusses the integration of real-world data using web APIs and IoT devices to synchronize dream environments.

Chapter 5: Learning from Feedback – Describes the feedback loop system and supervised learning to refine AI performance.

Chapter 6: The Ethics of Dream AI – Addresses ethical concerns, including privacy, data security, and responsible use of AI in dreams.

Chapter 7: Personalizing the Experience – Explains how clustering algorithms and machine learning are used to tailor dream environments to individual preferences.

Chapter 8: The Future of Integrated Worlds – Envisions future advancements, including brain-computer interfaces and enhanced emotional AI.

Chapter 9: Reflections on the Journey – Reflects on the impact of AI integration on personal and creative experiences, emphasizing ethical and personalization aspects.

Chapter 10: Beyond the Interface – Looks forward to continuous innovation and the ultimate vision of a harmonious blend of dreams and reality.

Together, these novels offer a rich narrative and technical exploration of integrating dreams with reality, showcasing the transformative potential of AI while addressing the associated challenges and ethical considerations.

www.ingramcontent.com/pod-product-compliance
Lightning Source LLC
Chambersburg PA
CBHW062111220526
45471CB00010B/3688